MW01715346

On the Upward Road

by

Richard V. Clearwaters

On the Upward Road

ON THE UPWARD ROAD

RICHARD V. CLEARWATERS
C/O CENTRAL SEMINARY
1250 West Broadway
Minneapolis, MN 55411

Library of Congress Catalog Card Number 91-67803

ISBN Number 0-9631570-0-0

Printed by Nystrom Publishing
9100 Cottonwood Lane
Maple Grove, MN 55369

Preface

Richard V. Clearwaters
1900 - Present

RICHARD V. CLEARWATERS, a soul-winning pastor, educator and author, said, "I am a Biblicist before I believe myself to be a Baptist." He dimensionalized the term and concept of a Biblicist when he defined it with the term "militant", thus giving Biblical content to the term "A Militant Biblicist" (Phil. 1:17b).

Within the annals of contemporary church history, it would be difficult to find a more unique trophy of the grace of God than Richard V. Clearwaters. Through this one, God has made an enduring impact upon the national and international direction of local churches, as well as mission boards and educational institutions. His academic achievements have become a legendary model of Biblical self-discipline and self-sacrifice. He is a graduate of Moody Bible Institute; B.A. Kalamazoo College; M.A. University of Chicago; ThG, B.D., D.D. Northern Baptist Theological Seminary; D.S.T. San Francisco Baptist Theological Seminary; D. Hum. Bob Jones University; and noted in the Marquis publication of "Who's Who in America".

It was on June 28, 1900, that Richard V. Clearwaters as one of eight was born into an obscure godly Methodist farming home in Wilmot, Kansas, subsequently moved to Nellie, Oklahoma, and in 1907 finally settled near Spokane, Washington. As the dullest of the eight, he squeaked through the eighth grade, refused to go to high school, and in 1916 he left his home to live the life of a prodigal son in the harvest fields, coal mines and lumber camps of Western Canada. In answer to his godly mother's prayers, he was wonderfully saved on December 10, 1921.

Within weeks of this date he responded to the call of God for full-time Christian service. Etched within the sunlit halls of memory, he recalls that as his mother was preparing breakfast he heard her singing, "The Ninety and Nine". As she sang, the words gripped his heart, and he responded to the Spirit's call. Thus it was on February 10, 1922, that he enrolled in the Moody Bible Institute and began a sixty-two year trek along that "rough and steep road into the desert to find His sheep." After two and one-half years he graduated from Moody as a Baptist by conviction.

In 1940 he was called as pastor of the influential Fourth Baptist Church of Minneapolis, Minnesota, a church which was founded in 1881 and epitomizing her motto: "Famous for the Gospel". His leadership influence as a militant Biblicist was felt throughout the State of Minnesota, but far beyond her borders nationally and internationally.

He led the Minnesota Baptist Convention out of the liberal Northern Baptist Convention. After the death of Dr. W.B. Riley in 1947 the Northwestern Schools, which Dr. Riley had founded, were divested of the Bible College and Seminary. Richard V. Clearwaters then founded Central Baptist Theological Seminary in 1956, as well as the radio voice of the Seminary, WCTS-FM, the Bible Station. His militant Biblicism caused him to triumph in a series of court battles. He then founded Pillsbury Baptist Bible College in Owatonna, Minnesota, in 1957. He gave Biblical leadership to the organizational structures which gave birth to the Conservative Baptist Fellowship, the Conservative Baptist Association of America, and the Conservative Baptist Foreign and Home Mission Societies. Faithful to the Bible as a militant Biblicist, he departed from these organizations when they departed from the Bible and espoused new evangelicalism. He led in establishing the New Testament Association of Independent Baptist Churches. Among the hundreds of Biblical treatises, pamphlets and books which he has authored, none are more widely read than *The Great Conservative Baptist Compromise, The Local Church of the New Testament, Ten Commandments* and *Stewardship Sermonettes.*

On April 4, 1982, Fourth Baptist Church of Minneapolis recognized Dr. Clearwaters' sixty-two years of service as a militant Biblicist, forty-two years of which were spent as its pastor. His favorite hymn, "My Task", was sung. He closed his final message from the Fourth Baptist pulpit with:

> I am walking on the upward way,
> For that still holds the sun;
> I am climbing the night pastures,
> Where the starry river runs.
> And if you seek to find me
> In my old and dark abode;

You'll find it written on the door
I'm on the upward road!

Dr. Clearwaters is now retired. After the severe illness and passing of his dear wife, he is residing in a retirement home and always enjoys fellowship with his many friends. He has enjoyed a very fruitful and blessed long life.

Dr. Clearwaters began this book in 1987 at the urging and encouragement of Mrs. Clearwaters and worked diligently writing much of the material until the illness and death of his wife in 1989. Later, he wished to complete the work and dedicate it to the memory of Mrs. Clearwaters. In late 1989 he directed and supervised this compilation of his writings and his life story taken from the many tapes of his messages through many years of preaching. Never taking notes or outlines to the pulpit, his style of preaching comes through this work very clearly. It is published for two reasons: one, to preserve for future generations the impact Dr. Clearwaters has had on the separatist and Biblical position of Baptists in the years past; and two, to inspire young people to understand that complete surrender to the will of God brings usefulness and blessing in God's service.

Many years ago, my father's dear friend, Dr. Harriet Bratrud, suggested he begin writing his autobiography. She offered to professionally commission its completion and arranged for an initial meeting with a major publisher out of state. After father learned of the large time commitment that was involved, he felt he didn't want to take the time away from the Church to start such a task, so didn't undertake this book until he was nearing retirement years. Special gratification goes to my parents' friend, Mrs. (Ralph) Evelyn Westphal, who spent many long hours of labor organizing and typing the original manuscript.

This book is about my father's lifelong commitment to the Lord, his family, the Fourth Baptist Church, education and causes. He gave me much of my outlook on life. He was a role model for me, both personally and professionally, and undoubtedly had much to do with my choice of a profession. He was my mentor, companion and friend. His sense of humor still sustains us both. Following is my father's story.

Jane L. Clearwaters

Dedication

This book is lovingly dedicated to the memory of my dear wife, Florence L. Clearwaters (February 6, 1910-April 10, 1989).

Born in Allegan, Michigan, on February 6, 1910, Florence L. Welch was raised among a family of several children. She received the Registered Nursing Degree from the Borgess Hospital School of Nursing in Kalamazoo where upon graduation she was employed by the City Health Department. It was during these years as a young adult that she came to a personal knowledge and acceptance of Christ as her Savior.

In April 1935 Florence L. Welch became Mrs. Richard V. Clearwaters, a distinction and role she cherished throughout her lifetime. She served the Lord in the home as mother of their daughter, Jane, and as a gracious, faithful help-meet to her husband for nearly fifty-four years.

Next to her love for her husband and family, Mrs. Clearwaters' ministry with the Seminettes and women's work of the church was of utmost importance. Her exemplary conduct as a dedicated and sacrificial pastor's wife was a constant and godly example, worthy of emulation before the student wives and women of the church. The Lord used her efforts to communicate to literally hundreds of women in a practical and Biblical way the values of a Christian home, life and ministry. In 1984 Central Baptist Theological Seminary conferred an honorary degree of Doctor of Humanities upon Mrs. Clearwaters for her outstanding contributions in this area.

Many lives were helped, encouraged and instructed through the life and ministry of Mrs. Clearwaters, for which we must praise and thank the Lord.

"Precious in the sight of the Lord is the death of his saints." Psa. 116:15

(The above is taken from the memorial program of the funeral of Mrs. Clearwaters on April 13, 1989.)

Mrs. Clearwaters.

Contents

Introduction

I don't believe that any school or organization is going to be a conservator of the faith; it'll have to be accomplished by a raising up of leaders. "There was a *man* sent from God, whose name was John." (John 1:6) There was a man sent from God, whose name was Moody, and others.

I read some time ago that an institution is a lengthened shadow of a man. I reflected on that. I presume that is true. I thought of Central Baptist Seminary organized in 1956. I thought of Pillsbury Baptist Bible College. Then I thought of the church where I have served for many years. These institutions are lengthened shadows of a man.

The lengthened shadow of a man has to be somewhat biographical. This is a reason for writing an autobiography. The danger in these writings, they tend to the worship of individuals. That's the trouble.

I want to state first of all the importance of the Bible, first in the life of the leader and then how it has extended itself into the whole program. "Thou hast honored thy word above all thy name." I always come back to that verse. The lengthened shadow of a man is the Word of God. When we began WCTS, I said, "It will be called the Bible station." The poet has said concerning the Bible:

> This is the golden casket where gems of truth are stored.
> It is a heaven-drawn picture of Christ the Living Word.
> It is the chart and compass that o'er life's surging sea
> Still guides through mists and rocks and quicksand,
> And still leads, O Christ, to Thee.

This has been my guide throughout my ministry. I've never had any doubt but that the Lord will let me know when my ministry is through. When anybody tries to play God in your life, or any group tries to play God in your life, you don't have to fear if you're positive you are in God's will. That's all you have to worry about. It's God's testimony He is protecting, and not you. This has been one of the greatest comforts in my life and given me more sweet sleep when other people worry.

> Behind my life the weaver stands to work His wondrous will.
> I leave it in His all-wise hands and trust His matchless skill.
> Sometimes He weaveth sorrow, and I in foolish pride
> Forget He sees the upper, and I the underside.

There is no tangled skein of life too difficult for His divine fingers if we are willing to cast it into His lap.

Chapter 1

Childhood Years

Parental Background

Three states, Kansas, Oklahoma, and Washington, contributed to the historical background of the Clearwaters family tree.

My father's family, Absalom Clearwaters, originally from Foley, Alabama, lived in the area of Champaign, Illinois. There were five children: Lee, Leonard, Ralph, Nathan Harrison Guy (my father), and a daughter, Harriett. Harriett died of tuberculosis in her 30s. I heard my father talk about how the family moved into a house where someone had died of tuberculosis. My father was in his teen years when the family moved to Kansas.

This large family put all of their earthly belongings on two covered wagons and started their trek westward for Kansas. Grandpa drove one team of mules, and Grandmother drove the other team of mules. They journeyed for days, sometimes sloshing through mud so deep up to the hubs of the wagon wheels. And when they came to the Mississippi River at Hannibal, Missouri, Grandpa leading the way looked down the bank of the river to the ferry below which would take them across the river. He got down from the wagon and went back to say to Grandma, "Sarah Jane, we had better turn around and go back home. It looks too dangerous." Sarah Jane replied, "We are not turning back; we are going to Kansas." And they went to Kansas.

My mother was one of four "Poe" daughters. Her mother's first husband (a Mr. Rogers) was a Civil War fatality. She married then a Mr. Poe, and was again widowed with four little girls: Anna, Susan, Hannah (my mother) and Nan. A severe tornado one year swept through Kansas in the area where they lived, and Grandmother took the little girls and sought refuge in the fence row where they were safe, but everything they owned, except the clothes on their backs and a half of a sheet, was destroyed.

Guy and Hannah Clearwaters—parents.

My father, Guy, and my mother, Hannah, met and were married in a little town by the name of Wilmot, a few miles from Winfield, Kansas. They were sharecroppers for a lawyer by the name of Will Lorton, who practiced law in Winfield. I was born at Wilmot, June 28, 1900, the fourth child in the family. The three older children were Ray, Bessie and Donald. The four younger children were Allen, born in Oklahoma, and Willis, Melvin and Weldon, all born in the State of Washington. Weldon, the youngest child, died in a farm accident when he was about eleven years old, June 19, 1920.

The Clearwaters family, 1915.

Homesteaders in Oklahoma

In the early spring of 1901 the Clearwaters family moved to live on a homestead of 160 acres near Nellie, Oklahoma, which was located about midway between Marlow, Lawton and Duncan. I was a babe in arms. When this territory was opening up for statehood in 1901, land was available free to people who wanted to homestead and who would pledge to stay for five years. More people applied than they had land to distribute, so a lottery was provided. My father was fortunate enough to receive a homestead in the lottery drawing.

During their first summer in the new land, they lived in a tent while they were digging and building their first permanent home which was a dugout. This was a basement with board walls, a well-constructed roof over it, and well-trenched on all sides to drain the rainfall away from the house. I remember some things about the dugout. You could hear the centipedes in the wall behind the boards that lined the dirt walls, running here and there. We didn't think anything of it at the time—they were just so many pets! I guess that was frontier life.

In the course of time they built a house with the same outside dimensions as the dugout. And although it was my pre-school days, I still remember how they used horses to pull the roof off the dugout and slide it up on poles to get it in place on the newly built house.

The reason they moved in early spring was so they could get a crop planted their first year. In the beginning, each homesteader had a very meager supply of farm equipment and horses, but they bartered and loaned and borrowed among themselves and managed to have a crop the first fall. Cotton was a cash crop which they sold at the cotton gin in Marlow.

I recall hearing my folks talk about a covenant they made with the Lord. They heard about the Oklahoma territory opening up, and my father promised the Lord that if He would give him a piece of land in the new territory, he would be a faithful witness for Him in this new community. For my father this was a bold promise, because by nature he was of a reticent personality and had only a second reader education and my mother a fifth reader education. As children they worked in the fields until things were frozen up in the fall, and as soon as it got thawed out in the spring, they worked again and went to school in the winter when they couldn't do anything else. My father was not given to public speaking, and he knew he had very little education, a very modest person. He considered himself to be a one-talented man, and he wasn't even sure what that was. He could read and write and had a good mind, but he was uneducated and he sensed it very keenly.

I remember hearing them talk about that covenant they made with the Lord. Though I was very young, I understood that a covenant was a promise you make to the Lord. They made this agreement with the Lord. And I shall always remember when we were children, even in arms, they would load us into a big lumber wagon and go across the prairie for miles to attend protracted meetings in a big brush arbor. They had no church building, no organized church, but the saints of God got together—the whole community would come together and have special meetings. They used itinerant preachers going through. The preacher carried a gun; they were hunters, for there was much wildlife in the territory.

Those meetings lasted four to six weeks. My father would take the team out of the field about three o'clock, bring them into the barn to feed and rest them before he would hitch them to the wagon to make the long drive with the family, old and young, to attend the services. The brush arbor was lighted for night meetings by each family bringing at least one kerosene lantern. These were hung on the walls, on the wide aisles and on the supporting posts in the center aisle. On Sunday everyone brought a basket lunch and ate on the ground. They then had an afternoon meeting and an evening meeting.

I was too young to know much about what was going on in that brush arbor, but I can remember very well, as though it was yesterday, when I was about five years old that I was lying on a straw bed covered by a tarpaulin under the stars in the bed of the wagon listening to the singing of the congregation.

> If you are tired of the load of your sin,
> Let Jesus come into your heart;
> If you desire a new life to begin,
> Let Jesus come into your heart.
> Just now, your doubtings give o'er;
> Just now, reject Him no more;
> Just now, throw open the door;
> Let Jesus come into your heart.
> (**Let Jesus Come Into Your Heart** *Mrs. C.H. Morris*)

As best I can remember, this was the beginning of my own conviction of sin. But I thank the Lord that conviction was fed by the testimony of a good father and mother who put the Lord first as best they knew how in their own lives and in their home. We had a family altar in the home. We also knew that when Sunday came, we would go to church. Have you heard of the disease, "Morbus Sabbaticus"? That means Sunday sickness. If we tried that on Dad or Mother, they treated the illness like any other through the week. Mother would say, "That's all right. Sick people ought to be in bed. You can't be up." You know when you're treated that way, you get well quickly! The folks never sent us to church; they took us to church. If company came, relatives or friends, to spend a Sunday, they were always invited to join the family in going to church. If not, they were invited to make themselves comfortable until we got home.

My father went to the school board and got permission to have a Sunday School in the schoolhouse. My father was elected superintendent, which position he held until the family moved to Washington in the spring of 1907. I remember well when we left there, when I was about six years old, my father, mother and all the children were asked to line up in front of the Sunday School. This little Sunday School band of people gave a big testimony of thanks to my father. It was eloquent how he carried out his covenant with the Lord! My father at that time was so overcome with emotion that he couldn't say anything, so my mother took over. She told the story how they promised the Lord when they came to Oklahoma they would do any reasonable service for the Lord if He would give them a home. They were faithful to their promise through the years.

They gave my father a big Bible, one of those pulpit Bibles containing the apochrypha (the ex-canonical books of the Bible). That Bible was in our family in a prominent place on the library table all through my childhood and young manhood. It was a testimony of my father's faith in the Word of God. I remember the Bible had a hasp on the side, because in those days that was the lockbox for the farmer where he kept all his legal papers.

That Bible became a very important book to me and at our family altar. I recall once ministering to an elderly woman in one of my first pastorates. She was unconscious when I got there. I was sent there by her sister. I went regularly and each time I recited the 23rd Psalm, hoping that she might have some consciousness. When she came to the place where she was able to recognize me and speak, she said how she thanked God for the 23rd Psalm. "When I was a little girl," she said, "I went to your Sunday School (this was in Kalamazoo, Michigan). I learned the 23rd Psalm." She was saved listening to the 23rd Psalm when she was coming out of a stroke.

That seed that is planted is the eternal Word of God. "Being born again, not of corruptible seed, but of incorruptible, by the word of God, which liveth and abideth for ever." (I Peter 1:23)

My mother and father were covenant-keeping people. They made a covenant with the Lord and kept it. They left conviction of sin with me and left me with the importance of keeping promises to God.

My first year in school was in Nellie, Oklahoma. Children did not go to school until they were six years old. It was a one-room schoolhouse teaching all eight grades. The one large room was rectangular in shape with a large platform in the front. The teacher's desk was located front center, which gave him a good view of the whole room. The most vivid memory I have of my first teacher was as a real disciplinarian. I saw him throw a bunch of keys the full length of the schoolroom at someone who was whispering in the back. They didn't whisper anymore. When those keys hit the floor, everybody knew he meant business! Sometimes those in the upper grades were twenty years old—they only went to school in the winter in the bad weather. They needed severe discipline to keep control over them. Older students many times were running teachers out of the schoolrooms. One time one committed some offense, and the teacher told him to go down to the creek and bring back a willow. He told him how big it should be. He brought it back, and then he stood on the platform and stooped over and the teacher laid that long willow on him until the willow was down to about two feet long. That was what they called corporal punishment. It was very severe discipline. I overheard my father and mother talking about him, and my mother said he suffered from neuralgia. I didn't know what that was, but I knew it made you have a very wicked disposition.

Each pupil had two slates hinged together, two inside surfaces for a permanent record and the outside for erasing. Each desk had an inkwell fitted into it, and each pupil kept a little wooden box in his desk containing two brown penny pencils with an eraser on the end, two more expensive yellow pencils, one with softer lead, one pen holder and two pen points, one fine for writing and one coarse for lettering or shading, and one twelve-inch ruler. Each student had a copybook, triple-lined to show capital letters. The teacher would put on the line above some slogan, like: "There's so much good in the worst of us, and so much bad in the best of us, there's no room for the rest of us." Such slogans we had to copy.

I was always at the foot of the class in writing. I had an excuse for that because I was naturally left handed. Prof. Thomas was not satisfied with that, so he tied my left hand behind my back during that exercise, and sure enough, I got so I could write with my right hand. The trouble was, you couldn't read either one, the left or the right. He wasn't such a great success in teaching penmanship! Later, however, in the schools in Washington, the teacher had the Spencerian method, supposed to be the easy-flowing type. Well, that didn't do me much good either. I can still write my name so it can be read. Maybe I should have done what William Rainy Harper did. He fell so much in love with Hebrew that he became lefthanded so he could write Hebrew from the right to the lefthand margin. Maybe I should have taken up something like that; at least it would have had a classical appearance!

The arithmetic book had examples of long and short division, addition, and subtraction and the multiplication tables.

The schoolroom was heated with a large pot-bellied stove, protected by a tin shield some five feet high, and on top a large pan kept filled with water. The stovepipe rose to the ceiling and angled to the farthest corner of the room to act as a radiator of heat. The schoolhouse was used for church services on Sunday.

Move to Washington

The climate in Oklahoma disagreed with my father's health. He suffered from rheumatism, and primarily for this reason the family decided to move to Washington state near Spokane. A public sale was advertised and in the spring of 1907 the family took an emigrant train on the Great Northern to Spokane, Washington.

My grandfather, Absalom Clearwaters, died before we moved from Oklahoma. My grandparent's place was near our place. Grandmother and her youngest son, Ralph, lived there, and both farms were sold out at the same time. Grandmother and Uncle Ralph went to Spokane, too, and Grandmother, Sarah Jane Weger Clearwaters, lived with us until her death in 1917.

As a result of the farm sale, father had the sum of $1800.00 with which to settle in the new country. This was quite an undertaking, changing locations with a large family and with no guarantee of anything in the new state.

An emigrant train is a stripped-down railroad train, the cheapest fare you could buy. We put two seats together, and the family (five children, the parents, one grandmother and Uncle Ralph) ate three meals a day on the train. We took baskets of food, and father would get off at a junction about every 300 miles to get supplies for his family. Grandmother would say, "Guy, where on earth are you taking us!"

I remember when we got to Spokane it was raining when we got off the train. The reason I know is because Grandmother had one lame foot and had to wear moccasins. We got off and it was dark, and I recall so well that she stepped in a pool of water. She said quite a few things about that—nothing for the record!

My father found a cheap hotel on Trent Avenue where we stayed our first night. My father's brother, Lee, lived on Moran Prairie. Our furniture was boxed, and Lee found a small house for rent near him on Moran Prairie. We rented on Moran Prairie in two different locations, and then father bought an eighty-acre farm about eight miles from Spokane. He bought the eighty acres for $3,000.00 from a maiden lady by the name of Sue Newman, so the home place before we owned it was called "The Newman Place". He paid for it as he took the crops off the land. It's interesting that my brother has since sold off the same land and much more at $500.00 an acre.

The house was quite inadequate for our family, and the barn was really nothing. It was a small building formerly used for chickens. My father bought a dismantled sawmill several miles up in the hills toward the mountain called Corral's Hill, or Lone Tree Mountain. The sawmill provided adequate dimension lumber to frame a large barn to house horses and cows on the main level and much storage for hay above. A machine shed was added under a lean-to roof which protected the farm machinery from the weather. On the house a T-structure of two floors and a full basement were added. This place became the "home place" for the family and its posterity.

This farm was ideal for a large family. In fact, my father once came home and told mother that he had advertised the place for sale.

This advertisement came out in the Spokane Spokesman Review:

"A BEAUTIFUL HOME

and one of the best dairy or mixed farm propositions in the country; only 2½ miles from city limits, paved and graveled road. 360 acres, 225 choice, black soil under cultivation, balance timber and pasture, good springs and running water, 90 acres winter wheat, 15 acres in alfalfa, 2 complete sets of buildings, one a beautiful seven room strictly modern house, except heat, with Delco lights in house and barn; large up to date barn, with stanchions for 25 cows, 8 horses and 50 to 60 tons hay; family orchard, lawn and shade.

This place is fully equipped and making good money; carries 41 cattle; now milking 20 cows; more shortly; has a retail dairy route, income about $500.00 per month; 8 fine work horses and harness; 50 tons of hay, and a complete dairy equipment for 50 cows; 3 autos, as well as a farming equipment and household goods; also 100 cords wood; personal property should be worth $10,000.00.

Owner is broken in health and must make a change by April 1st. The whole cheese goes for $40,000.00 and on terms, and when you know that the owner paid more than $500.00 per acre for 20 acres of this land you will begin to appreciate its possibilities and the bargain that he is now offering you.

G.N. LAND COMPANY, 316 HYDE BUILDING"

We children hearing about it asked mother where we will live when the place is sold. "What will we do with our horses, cows and other stock? How will we make a living without the farm?" Mother simply said, "The place is not sold yet. Don't worry about it until the time comes." Some weeks went by, and the talk about selling the farm died down. We asked mother again about what was happening. She said that when she asked father about it, he admitted that he had taken the farm off the market. Mother asked why he had changed his mind. He said that he kept reading his description of the farm until finally he said to himself, "This is just the kind of place I have always wanted!"

Fruit and vegetables were our livelihood. The orchards produced great varieties of fruit—summer and winter apples, apricots, peaches and pears. We would take it into the city and sell it. In the wintertime father and we boys would cut as much as a hundred cords of wood from our large pine and fir trees, which often grew five and six feet through. The sale of firewood made some financial income in the winter when there were no vegetables or fruit for sale. Sometimes we would hire one or two men to work at this all winter so the land would be cleared for plowing in the spring. Father also kept a large dairy herd, which provided a year-round income by the sale of milk and butter. Often the dairies on the near-side of Spokane would come for our milk. They would pay us 25 cents a gallon and retail it for 10 cents a quart. I didn't like farming—I never took to it. I wasn't good at it. I had a younger brother, two or three years younger than I. He was a carpenter, handy with his hands; he could do anything. He could work circles around me.

The worst evil influence over our lives as boys on the farm came from hired men. They would stay only a season and then move on. They were the most godless men, and my father many times would order some of them off the premises. These men would teach the boys evil practices.

Standing, left to right: Richard, Melvin and Donald. Sitting, left to right: Ray, Allen, Bessie and Willis.

The Clearwaters boys didn't always have a good reputation—they were known as "holy terrors" on the prairie.

We had seven boys and a girl in our family. My mother said she wouldn't take a million dollars for one of her children, but she wouldn't give a nickel for another one. I think she was speaking very sincerely. She didn't have any modern conveniences, and she made bread three times a week, did the sewing and housekeeping and washing for that many children besides an invalid grandmother. My uncle was with us for twenty years—came for Sunday dinner once and never went away! He seemed to like it real well! My uncle worked in the summer if it wasn't too hot. It was very strange—he was always there, a member of the family and yet really not. So that made twelve in the family.

My home had open doors to my father's mother until she died and to my mother's mother until she died. That impressed me. There's something about a relationship between a father and mother and their parents growing up with children. There's something taught there, more than you find printed in books. It has a very significant influence on children. We could probably find illustrations of the opposite all around us.

Land prices went up, and two professional men from Spokane (Bird and Stewart) wanted to become gentlemen farmers. They paid father $3,000.00 for the unimproved forty acres with no buildings. They made two or three attempts at farming and failed and finally sold their forty acres back to father for $1,000.00 less than they paid for it.

After father and the family moved away from the home place, it was occupied at different times by father's brother Leonard's family, as well as father's sons, Donald, Allen and Ray and their families. The home place, though unoccupied, is owned by the heirs of Donald, deceased since August 24, 1981.

From this home place it was two miles to the Moran Prairie country school. This was a large square building with four rooms, two grades were conducted in each room. It had three lady teachers and one male superintendent. As we walked to school, we had a choice of either taking the dirt and gravel wagon road or taking the Inland Empire Electric railroad tracks. It was a half mile from home to the nearest station on the railroad, Parkview, and then it was one-half mile to the schoolhouse from where we left the railroad track. All children in our family graduated from the eighth grade, except Weldon who died in his eleventh year.

Chapter 2

Prodigal Years

I am sorry to say that in Washington where we had only two grades in one room and one teacher, I was no better student than in Oklahoma where we had one room with eight grades. I was the poorest student of my mother's eight children. I disliked school very much. I was always delighted when something would cancel a day at school. They tried to teach me a little square root in the eighth grade. I never got that. I just kind of went over that. I got just a little over seventy, and they passed me, but I did not want to go to high school. My mother was visited by the professor who presided over the school. He predicted a great future for this one and for that one (there were eight in the family), and when he got to me, he said, "About Dick, I don't see much future about him. He's odd; he's strange; he's lefthanded, and not like the others." He was quite candid with her.

It was our parent's desire to have all of us children get a high school education. They made arrangements for all of us to go to the Lewis and Clark High School in Spokane. I had just squeaked through grade school, but I enrolled in Lewis and Clark High School. I only went one year.

In the fall of 1916 I was bored with school. One night I wrapped a few things in a mackinaw coat and hid the little pack along the road. The next morning I set off to go to school, but with only the clothes I wore and the little pack I had hid the night before, I got on a morning train and when nightfall came, I was in Canada. I became a prodigal son. I was sixteen years old; for five years I was a prodigal son.

I really wanted to live for the world, the flesh and the devil. I've often said, as I was sneaking out into the dark with all my possessions wrapped in that old mackinaw, if my folks had known that I was doing this, my mother would have come and said, "Now Son, we know that you're unhappy. We know that you do not appreciate this home and you want to leave. If you come here in the living room, tell your father and me just where we've failed in raising you. What should we have done that we haven't done? What did we do wrong?" If she had done that, I would have had to say, "No Mother; no Father, it isn't that. I simply want to live for the world, the flesh and the devil. There's nothing you could have done about it that would have changed those desires." The evidence of an unregenerate heart!

Arriving in Calgary, my first night I slept in a flophouse, the first one I was ever in. I might describe a flophouse for you briefly. It's just like a warehouse without any furnishings, but all of the floor is cut up with big chalk marks, marking off about three by seven feet, and you pay twenty-five cents a night for the privilege to sleep there on the floor. If you didn't have any blankets, you could use newspaper. If you had blankets, you tried to keep them close to yourself so you wouldn't get the livestock from someone sleeping along side of you.

I went to the employment agency and hired out as a harvest field worker and was employed at first near Vulcan, Alberta. One job was out near Lacombe on the Red River. In fact, there were two of us who went out there. The man's name was Bagley on the bench land of the Red River. It was late in the fall. He wanted two men. We got to Lacombe and had to walk fourteen miles to get there with our pack. We got there in time for dinner. I remember so well, this dear lady that fed us on biscuits. The other hired man and I kept digging into the biscuits, until finally she said, "That's all you shall have. The rest we're saving for morning." I remember that very well, because I never had heard that at home—that's the last biscuit you can have tonight, we'll save the rest for morning!

I was afraid of the winters in Canada. My first Canadian winter was in fifty and sixty degrees below zero weather working in the Brazeau Colleries coal mines in Nordeg, Alberta, north of Edmonton. On the way to Nordeg I took a side-door pullman—that's a boxcar with doors on the side! There were three of us travelers inside (we didn't even know each other's names), but on the way up, we had to race up and down inside the boxcar to get warm.

My first job there was digging ditches for the company town for more water in sub-zero weather. I got a little tired of that. I asked to quit, but they gave me a job inside the mine. We worked a mile underground on a vein of bituminous coal twenty feet deep. Two men could mine twenty tons in eight hours. They got paid according to how much they did. I drove a horse pulling empty cars in and full cars out from the face of the mine. This was much easier work than the miners who were used to hard work. The mine company furnished room and board for the workers in camps.

I just spent one winter there, and in the spring of 1918 I left the mine and went to work in the paper mills in Powell River, British Columbia, where I worked until the Armistice was signed on November 11, 1918. After the Armistice was signed, I went to Vancouver, British Columbia to work for the Whalen Paper Company, which sent me to Port Alice, British Columbia to work on one of their pulp mills. They cut spruce, hemlock and other trees, slid them into the ocean as trimmed logs in convenient lengths, and with chains made large booms and drew them to Port Alice, where they were made into snow-white pulp which was sold in those days to Japan for more than one hundred dollars per ton. The pulp is put over hot rollers and comes out as paper.

It was while working in the Port Alice pulp mill that I injured my right hand quite permanently in the rollers of the mill. I ended up in the hospital there in Port Alice. Nobody back home up to this time knew where I was. But a nurse who happened to be waiting on me in that hospital saw the record that my home had been in Spokane, and the name rang a bell with her, and it happened that she knew my mother. She wrote my mother, and I got a letter from my mother. The letter contained only one thing that I remember: "The way of the transgressor is hard."

I recall Mother telling me that she told the next door neighbor, Jake Sharp, a Copenhagen snuff-chewing trustee of the local Methodist Church, talking over the garden gate one day. "Jake," she said, "We heard from Dick." She told Jake where I was and what I had been doing—all about it. Then she said, "You know, Jake, I wrote and told him the way of the transgressor is hard." "Oh," he said, "that's too bad. You perhaps will never hear from him again. Hannah, that was the wrong thing to say. He'll never answer your letter." "Why, what's the matter with that, Jake?" "Well, that wouldn't encourage him." "Well," she said, "Those are not my words. Those are God's words. The way of the transgressor is hard. I can't make it easy—even God can't make it easy." That poor neighbor, who had churchianity but not too much Christianity, didn't have the faith in the Word of God that my mother had. She knew there was no place or time inappropriate for the testimony of what God said. In her heart she was led of the Spirit to remind me of something I already knew. It was hard, and getting harder every day!

She kept writing and begged me to come home for a visit. This led to my coming home. I went home with no intention of staying more than just a few days and leaving again. Prodigal sons form habits, acquire a vocabulary, do things that are not very fitting for a Christian environment. So I planned only on staying a little while, watching my vocabulary while I was there, doing a lot of listening and not much talking.

I remember when I first got home and saw my mother. I looked at her. My mother wasn't very tall, about shoulder high on me, and I said, "Mother, you're getting gray hair." And she said, "Son, you've made your part of them." She was doing some preaching then. She wasn't one who said it makes no difference what you've done. She was preaching all the time.

But while I was home, God intervened again. I was helping my father on the farm. We were hauling sand on a large lumber wagon, my brother Weldon and I. I stood up to urge the team, and he was sitting on one end of a board and I was sitting on the other end. When I stood up, he fell in front of the left front wheel of the wagon. I had urged the team, and I looked down just in time to see the wheel rolling over his body. He lived about a day and a half.

This tragedy hit me very hard. I shall never forget. I was under conviction before, but that was the beginning of the greatest depression I ever had in my life. Up to this time I had grown hardened to sin, but I saw the sorrow this brought to my folks. I remember they called the undertaker, and I went out a half mile to the road to meet the hearse to flag him down and lead him in. The next day while we were waiting a day for the funeral, a Christian Science woman, neighbor, found me out behind the barn, sitting there brooding, sorrowing, and she said, "I've taken this case in hand. Your brother is not dead. I want you not to be sorrowful about it." She said he is not dead! I looked at her to see if she had all her marbles. I had seen him die. I saw the mortician wrap him in the blanket. I saw them place that limp body in a wicker basket. I saw them load it in the back of the hearse. Then she stands and tells me he's not dead! Well, I didn't know what kind of religion that was, but it wasn't anything I wanted. I had to have something to keep my feet on the ground.

I felt to blame for the accident, though no one ever said that. This was the first grave dug in the family. In the night I often would kneel before an upstairs window looking out into the darkness until I went to sleep. I sometimes would walk as much as a mile in the woods and not remember anything. I really was greatly distressed. I came to the place where I had no brightness for which to hope in the coming of the morning. I had no fear of the night because I felt I had seen all the deep darkness could do.

I had a bedroom with only a thin wall from my father and mother. As I knelt with arms folded looking out the window into space, one night I overheard a conversation between my mother and father. My mother said, "Guy, I don't think you have slept a wink. What's the matter?" He said, "You know what's the matter. It's Weldon." He said, "You know, Hannah, I sometimes wonder if there is any God at all." That shook me more than anything I had ever heard. I thought it bad enough for me to have no faith, for me to be depressed, but here's my own father, a faith that I thought nothing would shake—it was like the rock of Gibraltar. By this my depression was deepened. Added to the natural sorrow of a death, I had caused my father to doubt his own faith. Here was my mother's answer: "Oh, Guy, don't say that. You know we gave each of our children to the Lord when they were born. Did we mean it? The Lord has taken one. We have seven left. We must trust Him now to help us take care of those left. If we deny Him, He may take the rest of them. He can take another one any time He wants. Did we dedicate these children to Him or not?" My mother preached one of the greatest sermons there in the darkness of the night.

After this experience, when I would go back to my window to gaze out into the darkness, the only cheer I could get for my sorrowing soul was the song of the cricket singing in the night. There was a little brook of water that ran in front of the house, and the frogs and the crickets were the only sounds we heard in the night. I recall now as I look back at a line in the poem, "The Acada" by Huxley: "Oh, thou harper of the night. I heard thy voice and hoped again." Imagine someone so depressed that the only joy they could think of was one of the most insignificant of God's creatures singing in the darkness of the night! After I was saved, I looked back and thought how foolish the mystery of iniquity makes people that they would be comforted by one of God's most miniature creatures like a cricket, when the open arms of the Son of God stand before them saying, "Come unto me, all ye that labor and are heavy laden, and I will give you rest." It is because of the ignorance of sin; it's because of man's indifference to the Gospel; it's because of man's peculiarity in doing his own thing selfishly. To keep me reminded of these days, a metal cricket has adorned my desk for years. I've never killed a cricket since I was saved.

Chapter 3

Conversion and God's Calling

This darkness continued from the middle of June 1920 to December 1921. I was under conviction, deep conviction. Sometimes I would plunge into sin; sometimes I would just withdraw and try to be alone.

One of the poets, William Ernest Henly, has written:

Out of the night which covers me,
Dark as the pit from pole to pole,
I thank whatever gods there be
For my unconquerable soul.

In the fell clutch of circumstance
I have not winced nor cried aloud,
And under bludgeons of chance,
My head is bloody, but unbowed.

It matters not how straight the gate,
Or charged with punishment the scroll.
I am the master of my fate.
I am the captain of my soul.

Oh, what braggadocia that is! Do you know what happened to William Ernest Henly? He committed suicide in his early 50s. Why? He was trying to be the captain of his soul. Nobody can be. Trying to be the master of his fate. Nobody can be. God has a purpose for every one of us. He promised David, "I will show thee the path of life." He has the promise for everyone who will accept it. William Ernest Henly refused to accept or ask God for that plan and that purpose. And like everybody else who fights God, he loses the battle. He ended up a suicide.

The Saviour's pleading I did not heed until December 10, 1921. It happened in an evangelistic meeting. A Holiness Methodist preacher from Dishman, Washington, was holding a two-week revival in the

Moran Prairie Methodist Church, Spokane, Washington in the 1920s.

Moran Prairie Methodist Church in 1990.

Moran Methodist Church. I have a picture of that church in front of my desk in my study. My mother planned to get me in every one of the meetings. I had been there every night. In fact the meetings were almost closed down because a great snowstorm came. The pastor and evangelist and about twenty people met in a little side room that Sunday morning to decide whether or not they should go another week. Some thought it would be no use. The preacher spoke up and said, "Well, the Lord led me to come over here, and we haven't had anybody saved. I don't like for us to let the devil beat us out. I'm willing to go on another week." They didn't tell him not to, so they went another week. The third week a fifteen-year-old girl, Wilma Goodrich, and myself were saved. Thank God! I often think of that meeting they had in that little side room debating whether they should go on another week. The Lord blessed it and I was saved. I always thought that was a challenge to people who get discouraged in soul-winning efforts. One wonders what might have happened had the meetings closed.

After the invitation was given, I went forward with my mother. I gave my heart to the Lord. Everybody present in the meeting gathered around the front and prayed, and when the evangelist had everyone give a testimony, he called on me. My first testimony was, "The Lord is my shepherd, I shall not want." I didn't even know I knew that verse!

I wish I could describe to the unborn child exactly what life is like in this world. Imagine yourself before you were born and someone tried to describe to you the new world you were going into—what you would see, and feel, and hear, and experience in your new world outside your mother. There would be no way on earth it could be done. It is an experience you have to have, that I had to have before I could understand it and it would become a part of me. It's exactly this way with those who are born again. The Word of God says:

> "And this is the condemnation, that light is come into the world, and men loved darkness rather than light, because their deeds were evil. For every one that doeth evil hateth the light, neither cometh to the light, lest his deeds should be reproved. But he that doeth truth cometh to the light, that his deeds may be made manifest, that they are wrought in God." John 3:19-21

When I was saved, I loved the things that I once hated, and I hated the things I once loved. It's an old story that you've heard perhaps about the veterinary who had brought to him a goat that had been eating old shoes and tin cans from the alleys. He developed a bad case of stomach trouble, and the veterinary decided the only thing to do was remove the stomach and give him another stomach. When he gave him another stomach, all this goat was interested in was the luscious pasture. In other words, he had a new set of tastes, his appetites were different, his wants were different. The things he once loved and ate had gone from him. "If any man be in Christ, he is a new creation: old things are passed away; behold, all things are become new." (II Cor. 5:17)

When I left the church, from the steps I threw a half-smoked pack of Chesterfields under a large tree in the church yard. Chesterfields had the slogan, "They satisfy", but they didn't satisfy me any longer! Many people believe in gradualism when it comes to worldly habits. They put off the cleansing.

The first testimony I gave was to my brother. We worked together, slept together. He was on one side of the bed putting on his clodhoppers, and I was dressing on the other side of the bed. I told him, "Don, I was saved last night." He dropped that shoe; I thought it would go right through the floor. "You were saved!" he said, "Well, I'll be damned!" I said, "You sure will if you don't accept Christ. You don't have any other choice." As we were walking to the field, he held out to me a box of Copenhagen snuff. I had used a box a day of that. He said, "Here have a chew." I said, "No, I don't want it." "Have a cigarette." I smoked thirty cigarettes a day. "No," I said, "I don't want it. I have no appetite for it." And he couldn't believe it. I had a new vocabulary—new appetites. Now that's conversion. There was no maybe, hope so, or think so—none of that. These firm decisions within twenty-four hours made a big difference in my life.

> When Jesus comes, the tempter's power is broken.
> When Jesus comes, the tears are wiped away.
> He takes the gloom and fills the life with glory.
> And all is changed when Jesus comes to stay.
> (**Then Jesus Came** *Smith-Rodeheaver*)

After serving the world, the flesh and the devil, I found myself driven and anxious to walk in the path of the Lord Jesus. I call that conversion. The Lord is able. He didn't do anything for me that He wouldn't do for anyone else. I don't believe there are any hopeless cases as long as one has a normal mind. He is not willing that any should perish.

I was marvelously saved. The Lord really delivered me. I made a resolution that I would serve the Lord just as hard as I had served the devil. If you try that, you have a pretty tough assignment; it was for me anyway. I did everything I knew how to do to be faithful. I was faithful in all the services. I was witnessing. I couldn't sing a note, but I even joined the choir! I did everything I knew how. But I did not realize that God was calling me to preach.

One morning my mother told me to go hitch up the buggy. "We are going to make a call on Mr. Powell." He had been to Mayo's, opened and closed with cancer, and he came home to die in about three months. My mother said I was to witness to him. When we were going over, I said to mother that I wouldn't know what to say to him. "Well," she said, "Just tell him what happened to you." I wondered all the way over what I would say. The thing that surprised me was when we got there, he opened the conversation. "Oh," he said, "I'm so glad you came. I heard what happened to you over at the church. I want to hear all about it." He had asked me for my testimony. So I told him the best I could what had happened. He accepted the Lord before we left.

It wasn't long after I was saved, early one morning I heard my mother singing downstairs. She was getting breakfast in the kitchen which was immediately beneath my bedroom. You know on the farm you do about two hours work before breakfast. As we used to say on the farm you take off your overalls at night and throw them on a nail, and when you reach for them the next morning, they're still swinging!

She was singing, "The Ninety and Nine". She had a clear natural soprano voice. She came to the last verse, "I will go to the desert to find my sheep." The Lord spoke to me in that verse. "Will you go?" And I without hesitation said, "Yes." My call was that simple and that sudden—as clear and as positive as my salvation experience. You would be surprised how many seminarians today do not have a clear call to the ministry. That's why we find so many "also rans". There are far less young people going into the ministry today. It seems to be dying out.

The next Sunday when I went to church, a deaconess in the Methodist faith, who wore one of these little black headpieces, came up to me in the back of the auditorium and said, "Has it ever occurred to you that the Lord might want you in the ministry?" I answered, "Yes, Eva, the Lord has spoken to me." She said, "Then don't hesitate to get off to school right away, because," she said, "so many have this call and they put it off and they wind up not obeying the Lord." The Lord sent her to talk to me immediately. She recommended I go to a Holiness Methodist school in Chicago, the Chicago Evangelistic Institute on Washington Boulevard (when I got to Chicago I visited this school).

I had a brother-in-law who had attended Moody Bible Institute for five terms and was in the Presbyterian ministry. So I went to his place. I talked to them, and he and my sister suggested that maybe the Lord was calling me to go to Moody Bible Institute. I was convicted by that, and I thought maybe that was the answer.

I went home from that meeting with them and took a bus out as far as I could go and walked about a mile more, to go to the local cemetery where my youngest brother was buried. It was winter, February, in kind of a blizzard. I walked to the cemetery and went in the gate and bowed there at my brother's grave. I said, "Lord, I'm not very much, but what I have and what I am I'm willing to give it to you. Thank you for salvation."

This was a very difficult decision for me because I thought you had to be educated, and I had a very poor record in school. No one ever had a lower self-esteem than I had—before I was saved and after I was saved. I felt I was so happy to be saved, if the Lord would just leave me alone to enjoy salvation. I couldn't see any way, but nevertheless I made my resolution with the Lord.

I have often turned to the 40th Psalm in time of joy and in time of crisis. Many times I have read this Psalm on my knees and claimed every bit of it, as the Lord claimed me and my witness for Him.

> "I waited patiently for the Lord; and he inclined unto me, and heard my cry. He brought me up also out of a horrible pit, out of the miry clay, and set my feet upon a rock, and established my goings.
>
> "And he hath put a new song in my mouth, even praise unto our God: many shall see it, and fear, and shall trust in the Lord.
>
> "Blessed is that man that maketh the Lord his trust, and respecteth not the proud, nor such as turn aside to lies.
>
> "Many, O Lord my God, are thy wonderful works which thou hast done, and thy thoughts which are to us-ward: they cannot be reckoned up in order unto thee: if I would declare and speak of them, they are more than can be numbered.
>
> "Sacrifice and offering thou didst not desire; mine ears hast thou opened: burnt offering and sin offering hast thou not required.
>
> "Then said I, Lo, I come: in the volume of the book it is written of me,
>
> "I delight to do thy will, O my God: yea, thy law is within my heart.
>
> "I have preached righteousness in the great congregation: lo, I have not refrained my lips, O Lord, thou knowest.
>
> "I have not hid thy righteousness within my heart; I have declared thy faithfulness and thy salvation: I have not concealed thy lovingkindness and thy truth from the great congregation.
>
> "Withhold not thou thy tender mercies from me, O Lord: let thy lovingkindness and thy truth continually preserve me.
>
> "For innumerable evils have compassed me about: Mine iniquities have taken hold upon me, so that I am not able to look up; they are more than the hairs of mine head: therefore my heart faileth me.
>
> "Be pleased, O Lord, to deliver me: O Lord, make haste to help me.
>
> "Let them be ashamed and confounded together that seek after my soul to destroy it; let them be driven backward and put to shame that wish me evil.
>
> "Let them be desolate for a reward of their shame that say unto me, Aha, aha.
>
> "Let all those that seek thee rejoice and be glad in thee: let such as love thy salvation say continually, The Lord be magnified.
>
> "But I am poor and needy; yet the Lord thinketh upon me: thou art my help and my deliverer; make no tarrying, O my God." (Psalm 40)

He sent me out to be a minister of the Gospel. Nobody could believe it. But it was God's will. How could one who had no interest in the Bible, who knew nothing about the Bible, how could he have such a drive that he would learn over one hundred chapters by heart! All things becoming new!

Two things stood at the beginning of my Christian life that have been a steadying force throughout my complete Christian life. One, I was soundly saved and knew it and never doubted it—never had any question about my salvation, about being born again. That is one thing in Christian service that one should be dead sure of. No trumpet of uncertain sound is going to be heard for very long. The second thing was my call to the ministry. I was definitely called to the ministry in a very unique way. From the time I was saved I made a vow with the Lord that I would perform any reasonable service. I would try as hard to serve the Lord in every way as I had been serving the devil.

Chapter 4

Education

Moody Bible Institute

I went home and told my father that I felt called to the ministry. "I'm thinking of going to Moody Bible Institute to study." He said, "You better wait six months." He had a tremendous lot of common sense and he was smart enough to know that only a series of miracles could ever make anything out of me.

You know, there's nothing more dangerous than for someone to wait when the Lord has talked to them. The devil can talk you out of it, and he can use born-again Christians to talk you out of it. He can use someone who loves you very dearly to talk you out of it. There wasn't any chance in the world that I would wait six months. If I had waited six months, I perhaps would never have come into the ministry.

I went to the pastor of the church, and he wasn't for it at all, and I knew he was dead wrong too! I said to my father, "Well, the Lord has called me, and the kingdom task requires haste. I'm going to leave." And so I did.

Another thing that was very hard for me, there were seven boys and a girl in our family, and I had demonstrated through all the years that I was the dullest in school of all of them. Now that is the truth. I was like the little boy that went home and his mother was after him all the time and said, "Why do you have to be at the foot of the class all the time?" "Well," he said, "Mother, what's the difference," he said, "they teach the same thing there as they do at the head of the class." But what was on my side was, "If any man be in Christ, he is a new creation; old things pass away." In other words, my dull mind became a normal mind. I wasn't any smarter than anybody else, but I don't think I was much duller either. The·Lord did that for me. This is something many folk get intimidated about. They say, "I can't." That's the wrong thing to say.

One of the principles that dominated my life after I was saved was, "Where God will guide, He will provide." I felt very inadequate because of my schooling, but I did believe from the beginning that where God will guide, He will provide. I never was moved from that. Another principle which has dominated my life is that God has a plan for me, and He is anxious for me to have it—more anxious than I—and that if I cooperate with Him, I could know what that plan is.

My call was to win souls to Jesus Christ—nothing fuzzy about it, nothing professional about it, nothing remote or indirect about it. God called me to save souls.

I was preaching at Pillsbury College one time, and a lady came up to me and said, "You said something once that I will never forget." Well, I wondered what it was. Maybe I've said some things I would like to have people forget! She said, "Well, you were so convinced of the Lord's leading in your life, what He wanted you to do and when He wanted you to do it, that you just hoped nobody would get in your way, because they wouldn't have much chance of stopping you." I have felt that way all my life.

As I was leaving my mother gave me my youngest brother's little testament he had earned in Sunday School. This was a memorial to me that I was going to substitute a life that had been taken out in very early years.

Of course, I had no high school education. When I went to Chicago to Moody Bible Institute, I didn't expect that I'd get more than a Bible

Institute education, and go out then and look for a little church and go on from there. That was what I expected to do.

Only six weeks old a Christian, I traveled to Chicago to go to Moody Bible Institute. I came to Chicago in the time of the breadlines in 1922. With one well-worn suit and all my earthly possessions in a 75-cent suitcase and $17.50 in my pocket, I arrived in Chicago for an education.

I walked from Union Station to where State and Madison meet. I had heard that was the busiest corner in the world. I upended my 75-cent suitcase and sat down on it by the side of the building. I sat there to watch the traffic. A big Chicago cop came along and walked by me a couple of times. I guess he thought I needed help. He said, "Young man, are you traveling?" I said, "Yes, sir, I'm traveling. I'm on my way to the Moody Bible Institute. Where will I get a street car?" He told me where and went on by. He came back later, and I was still sitting there. "You seem to be interested in this corner," he said. "I am," I said. "I heard about this corner. It's one of the busiest corners in the world." He said, "Well, there are no dull moments here. I served at this corner many years." So I talked to him about his soul. He just looked at me as if to say, "You're just one of them!" I didn't get very far, but I tried.

When I got to the Moody Bible Institute, they said, "We do not find an application for you in our files." "An application," I said. I had not thought of that! They gave me one to fill out and told me how many weeks it would be before the new semester would begin. They assigned me a room and sent me to the school's employment office. I got a job as a dishwasher in the school kitchen. My room was in the 153 Building, where I continued to live even when I entered school in the spring semester.

I had $17.50 in my pocket when I got to Chicago and no financial angel. I had left a motorcycle at home in the shed, and I thought maybe some time my brothers would sell it, and I might get a little windfall from it. Well, I didn't know until two years later they had sold it, but forgot to send me the money! Nobody helped me. I was on my own. My school bill for board and room was $8.40 per week. One of my first jobs was as a busboy in the Marshall Field tearoom for $6.00 a week. I had to pray in at least $2.40 per week, which did not include my carfare to work, so in all kinds of weather I walked to and from work. I served two and three stations in the tearoom, carrying away used dishes and bringing in glasses and silver. If the waitresses' tips were good, they shared them with the busboys. This is where I made my $2.40 per week deficit.

One day going down on the elevator from work in the Marshall Field tearoom, a boy asked me if I was a tither. He worked with me in the tearoom and received $6.00 a week like I did. I said, "No, but if I ever get on my feet, I expect to begin tithing." About this time the elevator was stopping on the main floor, and as we got out he said, "That is what I have been waiting for, too." We shook hands, and I said, "You just made a tither out of me." He said he did not understand. I said, "Your answer is what hit me, that you were waiting for the same thing. I reasoned immediately that I would get on my feet a lot quicker by being obedient to the Lord than I would in disobedience." He made a tither out of me.

As time went on I had to change work to get in all my classes. I operated an elevator on the gold coast for $105.00 per month, 8 hours a day, 7 days a week. I sold Knap-Welt shoes; I sold Fuller brushes; I sold Oriental rugs; I did various kinds of kitchen work. In the Institute kitchen my official title was "Third Cook". (Chief Cook and Pastry Cook were first and second.) In this position I was really a swing-cook, taking the place of the two others above me when they were on vacation or sick.

Two things I remember about those days in the Institute kitchen. I worked with a young lady named Miss Van Ess. We worked under a chief cook who was unsaved—a strange thing in the Institute kitchen. The third person I worked with was a professing Christian but had a very poor testimony. His name was Workman. He was the bookkeeper who took care of the finances in the kitchen. This girl and I were always trying to straighten out the lives of these two other employees. A new Christian is always tested. My daily work was also a daily witness to my closest associates. It was a natural thing.

My employment during school days was most necessary to pay the bills for my education, but I am certain that the Lord who provided the financial means for my training also made my employment a definite part of my education.

Judson had a rule of life to spend no minute in idleness. That wasn't hard for me to follow. We had always worked hard, summer and winter, on the farm. I had never played sandlot baseball. I'd never been on a team or league of any kind. We worked through vacations and when we were out of school. So I spent my extra time memorizing Scripture. I used to walk to Oak Street beach along Lake Michigan memorizing Scripture. I put a great deal of emphasis on memorizing the English Bible. I felt a tremendous deficiency in learning, and I knew this was the book that was important. It was the book that had brought me to where I was, and so I gave myself to that task. I've always been grateful that I did that. When I left the Institute after two and a half years, I had learned one out of ten verses in the Bible by heart, one-tenth of the English Bible in the King James Version. My folks used the King James in the family altar, and I naturally memorized Scripture from the King James. This was a great help to me and a great testimony to my own soul.

In the Bible Institute we got all kinds of experience: street preaching, missions, sanitariums, hospitals, jails, railroad shops at noon. We preached and witnessed and gave out tracts and did personal work in all places. This is where I began. A Bible Institute stresses three things: one, they teach the English Bible; two, they teach gospel music; and three, they teach evangelism. If you would go across the country to find some of the outstanding large churches today, you would find that many of them were started by Bible Institute graduates. Why? Because of the emphasis on the Word of God.

I was a student in the Moody Bible Institute from February 1922 to July 1924. I want to mention the deposits that my professors, both great and near great, left in me. Dr. James M. Gray was President of the Moody Bible Institute and taught Synthetic Studies of the Bible, which required the student to learn a general outline of every book of the Bible. For example, Genesis was summarized with eight words: creation, fall, flood, nations, Abraham, Isaac, Jacob and Joseph. A book by this title is published today by the same author, who also taught Bible Exegesis.

Dr. C.P. Meeker was Professor of Evangelism, and he took us through Reuben Archer Torrey's book, *How to Work for Christ*, and we had to memorize hundreds of verses as we studied how to deal with different types of lost sinners, answering their questions and objections from the Bible, giving chapter and verse.

Dr. John Page taught Bible Doctrine and used Reuben Archer Torrey's book, *What the Bible Teaches*, and we were required to learn major Bible verses with chapter and verse. Incidentally, Dr. Torrey was

D.L. Moody's Superintendent and Master of Curriculum.

Robert Dick Wilson from Princeton Seminary, conversant with seven languages, was a frequent lecturer at Moody, with R.A. Torrey and Dr. Louis Evans, who had memorized the whole New Testament. The Founders' Week Conference brought Bible scholars from around the world—Duff Forbes from Australia, G. Campbell Morgan and W.H. Griffith Thomas from England, and evangelists such as Billy Sunday, Paul Rader and William Edward Biederwolf.

When I went to Chicago to Moody Bible Institute, I didn't expect that I'd get more than a Bible Institute education and go out and look for a little church and go on from there. In answer to my prayers, I finally got a "call" to a church while I was a student. It was a Federated Church at Wilton Center, Illinois, about half way between Kankakee and Joliet. After a three-month trial, they promised me $1,000 per year, but they never quite made it. It was half Baptist and half Methodist (a Methodist church in a Baptist building), supported by a rural community. I was there over three years. I went on Friday night for prayer meeting. Then I did my visiting on Saturday and had services on Sunday.

Northern Baptist Seminary

The week of graduation from Moody Bible Institute, Dr. Shaffer, the Dean of Men, called me into his office. I wondered what I had done wrong. He said, "What are your plans?" I said, "Well, if I can find some little church that will have me, I am going into the pastorate." He said, "I think you are making a mistake. I think you should go on to school." He said, "Aren't you a Baptist?" I had been baptized at the First Baptist Church of Spokane when I was home on vacation. He said, "I think if you let me call up Northern Baptist Seminary, they will on my recommendation take you as a special student." I told him that I did not have a high school education. He said, "That does not need to stop you."

He told me to go down to a certain place in downtown Chicago where the University of Illinois gave entrance examinations for high school four times a year. He said, "You go down there, and they will tell you what books to read and then you take the examinations. And I don't think you'll have to go to high school."

So I took his advice. In six months while attending Northern Baptist

Early pictures in school and seminary.

Seminary I completed four years of high school education. I went down evenings and got the assignments, and I hired a faculty member of Northern Seminary to teach me mathematics (I never had a mathematical mind) ten evenings, three hours an evening. I paid him $1.00 an hour—big money in those days. He was glad to get it. He needed money, and I needed help. I took the examinations and had a handful of cards to show that I had passed; and so completed four years of high school. Those cards were on the authority of the University of Illinois—they couldn't be denied anywhere.

Before I was saved my mother said I was the dullest of her eight children! In nine years in Chicago I completed twelve years of schooling and acquired five earned degrees. There was only one way that was possible: "If any man be in Christ, he is a new creature!" Take God at His word. Paul Rader had a sign in his tabernacle which I shall never forget: "Let go and let God." I attended his tabernacle often when I went to Moody Bible Institute. I shall never forget that sign, because it was exactly what I did, the best I knew how, when I accepted Christ.

I attended Northern Baptist Theological Seminary at 3040 Washington Boulevard, in Chicago, as a special student on Dr. Shaffer's recommendation. The seminary at that time also had a four-year theological college. The school did not limit how many hours a student could take if he had a certain grade average, and I took as many as thirty class hours per semester. In Bible Institute you learn the English Bible. In seminary you not only learn the Bible, but you learn a lot of things about the Bible and its inter-relationships. I was very happy studying. I was challenged every hour I was there. Many students never finish their education because they get married too soon and start having children. I often went through a nine-month term of school without any social life that could be called dates.

The strangest thing happened while I was at Northern Baptist Seminary. I still didn't have my high school finished when the president called me in and said the professor of English diction is not going to be back the rest of the year. He was sick, and there were six weeks yet of the term. He wanted me to take the class as a substitute. So I was teaching college diction as a substitute before I had my high school education. The standards have changed a lot since then!

In my studies I ran across a psychologist named William James. My knowledge of him did more for me than any other psychologist. This was the time when the study of psychology was coming in. Many students didn't know the minor prophets as well as they knew the psychologists of the day! William James made probably the greatest contribution to my thinking of any single psychologist with which I am familiar. I have most of the major ones on my shelf.

William James believed that all normal minds have equal retentive powers; they differ only in degrees of interest and methods of learning. I think that's a substantial statement and could be demonstrated many times. All normal minds, and we all like to think we are normal, have equal retentive powers, but differ only in degrees of interest and methods of learning. Many might say, I was cheated, I was born that way, I was only a farm boy. But when I was saved, I had a burning desire to prepare myself for the gospel ministry. I knew I wouldn't be very effective as a soul winner without preparation. My mother used to say, "You don't even go to the timber to cut wood without sharpening your ax." You might get a few trees down and you might get a little wood, but you would not be very effective.

All normal minds have equal retentive powers; they differ only in degrees of interest and methods of learning. I recall the first time I tried to preach. I was in a rescue mission, Bible Rescue Mission on West Madison Street. I was preaching on Isaiah 53:6, and I carried with me an outline sheet of notes. I got through that outline in about five minutes! I promised the Lord then I would never do that again, and I have never taken notes with me to preach since. I would have been embarrassed if I had not had a testimony. I just closed the Bible and notes and gave my testimony. It was spontaneous. I had something to say; I had a message. I could tell others what Christ had done for me. When I got away from the notes and gave my testimony, we had souls saved and I thank God for that.

I attended Northern Baptist Seminary when it was an unaccredited institution. It was only thirteen years old when I enrolled. I carried away four years of work which was equal to six or seven years of work—I took just about everything they had. I took thirty hours the last year I was there. In fact, I earned a $625.00 scholarship to Colgate University.

Here again I want to mention some of the men who had a great impact on my education. A.T. Robertson, a national authority on the Greek text of the New Testament, lectured regularly at the Northern Baptist Theological Seminary. I studied there under a faculty that obtained their higher education from two schools: Rochester Theological Seminary and the Southern Baptist Theological Seminary of Louisville, Kentucky. The Rochester School was built around Augustus Hopkins Strong. And his devotees on the Northern Seminary faculty warned us against Dr. Strong's theistic evolution tendencies and his belief in Ethical Monism.

Dr. Jacob Heindricks was as conversant in German as he was in English, and he taught Theology and Old Testament courses. Julius Robert Mantey, a joint author of the *Dana-Mantey Greek Grammar*, was the head of the New Testament Department.

James Moffat, from Union Seminary of New York, a professor and New Testament translator, was a frequent lecturer at Northern Seminary, as was Dr. Harry Ironside, who also lectured at Moody Bible Institute.

Colgate University/Kalamazoo College

I took the $625.00 scholarship out to Colgate University in New York. When I came to see the Registrar, a Mr. Howlet, I brought my credits with me and I had my transcript sent ahead. I will never forget, he looked at my high school cards and then at me and said, "You're another one of those short-cut men. The fewer we have of them the better we like it." I said, "I don't know if I understand what you mean." "Well," he said, "that's just what I mean. You will have to take another year of mathematics." The Northern Association of Schools required another year of mathematics. Well, right then and there our friendship ended! I had struggled through plain geometry, and I was never good in mathematics, and by taking it by entrance examinations that didn't make it any sweeter to Mr. Howlet. I didn't feel led to take more mathematics!

So I asked to see the President of Colgate. Howlet said that he was very busy and could not see me. I walked away from there, and I saw a sign which read, "George Cutten, President". I asked his secretary if he was in. She said, "Yes." I said, "Well, I would like to talk to him a little bit about his book on psychology." "Oh," she said, "he would be glad to talk to you about that." So I went in, and we talked a little bit about the book, but much more about something else! He ended up taking me down to Colgate Inn for a lovely big steak while he listened to me. He saw my problem. He told me the North Central Association of Schools did not require the extra mathematics, and he offered to call Kalamazoo College in Kalamazoo, Michigan, and recommend me there for enrollment. That's where I ended up. However, Kalamazoo College honored only $75.00 of my scholarship!

In the late summer of 1928 I resigned my Wilton Center Federated Church, where I had pastored during my student days, and I moved to Kalamazoo, Michigan to enroll in Kalamazoo College. I had earned from Northern Baptist Theological Seminary a Th.G and Th.B and B.D.

Kalamazoo College was a highly regarded Baptist school, an excellent academic college on the international standard of accreditation, but very liberal. The proud boast of the school was that half or more of their faculty were Harvard or Yale trained. They emphasized that the students be exposed to the five great philosophies that dominated civilization from the birth of Socrates to the death of Jesus: Epicurean, Stoic, Platonic, Aristotelian, and the Christian philosophy and spirit of LOVE. In literature Professor Mark Bailey was the head of the Romance Language Department, and Professor Milton Simpson, a devotee of William Lyons Phelps of Yale University, was the head of the Literature Department. He still insisted on much memory work in this field. The Greek and Latin Classics were each given a semester.

In the classroom they would have slogans in Greek and Latin. Even my degree was written in Latin. It was quite an honor to go to Kalamazoo College, and you only went on approval and on the condition of equalling or bettering your transcript grades. They looked down on people trained in fundamental schools.

They laughed at my credits and transcript—all non-accredited, they said. I said, "But will you receive me as a student?" "Yes, but you will be in the freshman class." Mr. Bacon, the Registrar, said if I did as well or better there as I did where I came from, they would receive my credits at par. I said, "Mr. Bacon, will you please put that in writing?" "Very gladly," he said (he didn't mean it, though), and I treasured that piece of paper and made pretty sure that I did a little better! I was a freshman one year, and I graduated the next year with honors and had a scholarship to the University of Chicago. That sounds like boasting, but it's the truth.

That scholarship was precious in those days because it was in the depression. My roommate brought eggs from the country once a week, and I bought rusk to go with it; that was our meal.

I don't talk down accreditation, but neither do I think it is any sacred cow. This is another affliction that people suffer from now. They think they have to go to an accredited school. We fought that ever since we established Pillsbury College. If one wants to be a doctor or a teacher or anything else, I think that he should have at least a year in Bible college if he's going to be a Christian doctor or teacher. That's hard to get through the heads of parents and young people. This is a day when it seems that the accreditation boogie is on all the horizons. Napoleon asked only one question before someone was going to be promoted. They would say, "Well, he graduated from the military school in Paris with highest honors, etc." Napoleon said, "Save your speech; I want to ask you one question, what has he done?" That pricked the balloon. If you have gone mad over accredited institutions, God help you; because you are going to have to accredit yourself. If you aren't able to do that, I would't give a dime for your transcript; in other words, if you can't deliver the goods. Everyone has to accredit himself. You might have a chain of degrees as long as a log chain after your name. I had five earned degrees when my wife and I went to our first pastorate, and we were promised $150.00 a month. Degrees don't accredit anybody. That's a backdoor entrance.

I recall speaking at the 35th anniversary of the Northern Baptist Seminary, and afterward a couple came up to me. They had gone to school four years and got a degree from a non-accredited institution in Minneapolis. They said, "Why didn't you tell us that institution was not accredited?" I said, "Did that change your education?" They were then enrolled in Northern Baptist Seminary. I said, "Why are you wasting your time here? I came here when this school was only thirteen years old and it was non-accredited. It was bearing the reproach of the whole denomination. Did the Lord lead you here or not?"

When I was leaving Kalamazoo College, I was in the President's office, Charles Goodsell, and he said, "I've been wanting to talk to you, Dick." He said, "You don't mind me calling you by your nickname." I said, "No, I'll just call you Charlie!" He had just handed me my degree; I had earned it. My graduation was over, and I was on my way. I knew he was a died-in-the-wool modernist. He said, "Now, Dick, you're going to Chicago University." I said, "That's right." He said, "Why do you want to go to Chicago University?" I said, "For more education." He said, "You're just as much a fundamentalist now as you were when you came here. We haven't changed you a bit." I said, "Now listen, Charlie, do you still recommend modernism? How can you honestly sit in that President's chair and recommend to me, just going out into my ministry, modernism which has failed you." I named the pastorates where he had failed; they were giving him a gold watch and chain to leave every place he went. He finally got a professor's chair in a college! Incidentally, he died sitting in the President's chair in a chapel service. I said, "If I sat there and was honest, I would at least be neutral. I couldn't recommend something that had failed me." "Well," he said, "I see that I'm not going to help you any."

He felt real badly that he couldn't change me. You know, it is a religion with them to knock the faith out of you and give you their philosophy of liberalism. That is their purpose. No difference how big a dummy you are, if you go along with them, they put their stamp on you and put you in high places. I only attended one year.

It is supposed to be intellectual to be doubting and to look down upon the plain teaching of the Word of God and the doctrines of the inspiration of the Bible, the deity of Christ, the virgin birth and blood atonement. It doesn't take intellectualism to deny those things. The fool hath said in his heart there is no god. You don't need to worry about men you will meet like that. Pray for them and hope they will get saved before they die and go to hell. This is the kind of courage you are going to have to have. A verse in Hebrews says we will go with Him without the camp bearing His reproach. You look around among leaders that have amounted to anything and see if any of them are marching around without any scars. They might look nice on the parade ground, but if you are going to amount to anything for Christ and the Word of God in these days, I want you to know that you're going to have to go with Him without the camp and bear His reproach. Christians have never been in the majority.

Chicago University

I went to Chicago University. I had decided what I wanted to take. The Dean pushed it aside and looked at me over his silver spectacles (he looked over them more than he looked through them) and said, "Now, young man, the essential thing in enrolling in this institution is that you get our point of view." I said, "Perchance do you mean the historical approach to religion?" I was a scholarship student, and I had always wanted to go to Chicago University. Then I said to him, "I'm losing my desire to go to this school." He said, "Why?" I said, "I can't even get enrolled but the Dean wants to cram something down my throat. It has violated the principle that attracted me here." He said, "What is that?" "That this is the place of untrammeled thought." He got up from his beautiful desk and walked around and put his hand on my shoulder and said, "Young man, this is the place of untrammeled thought. Those are my words." Of course, I knew that.

Fundamentalists could never be half as dogmatic or prejudiced as modernists. When one is prejudiced against the Word of God, this book says that God sends them strong delusions that they should believe a lie. This makes them more absolutely egotistical and more unbending than any fundamentalist ever dared be. We are said to be opinionated; we are called dogmatic! We don't know how to be opinionated and dogmatic like a modernist who denies the Word of God. God sends them strong delusion that they believe a lie. We are filled with the Holy Spirit and believe the holy truth. So you see, we don't ever need to worry. There's nothing new about skepticism and infidelity, and I want to say, you haven't seen anything yet.

I enjoyed my work at Chicago University. Edgar Johnson Goodspeed was the head of the New Testament Department, and J.M.P. Smith the head of the Old Testament Department. Robert Maynard Hutchins was the President of the University, assisted by Mortimer Adler. These two occasionally held forums on the campus for the benefit and participation of the faculty and students. Mortimer Adler did not believe in biological evolution, and when he was challenged by it, he would say, "No, I do not believe in evolution. I am a scientist, and when you give me objective evidence that I can observe, collect and classify and interpret as objective facts, I will consider the theory of evolution."

Dr. Hutchins later resigned the presidency of the University and joined the so-called "think tank" of California. Another faculty member was Shirley Jackson Case who was an acknowledged historian, but was already beginning to indulge in the "subjective reconstruction" of history. "Subjective reconstruction of history" is a deceiving thing. It means they do not report the questionable and the uncertain because that might not convince many people. They smooth over the truth.

I took my graduate degree under Dr. Goodspeed in the field of Greek New Testament literature. I wrote my Master's on the influence of Ethiopic Enoch on the Greek Apocalypse of John in parallel columns. It was a contribution to knowledge according to Dr. Goodspeed. When I was going to write on that subject, Goodspeed tried to talk me out of it. He had more faith than he wanted people to know about, and he didn't want a fundamentalist to have a subject that would prove anything against liberalism. I received the degree of Master of Arts August 28, 1931.

I wanted to fulfill the qualifications for a Ph.D. I re-enrolled for the Ph.D., but ran out of money six months before I got the degree. At that time for a doctor's degree one may have had to go to London and spend three months in residence, or one may have had to go to Chile. Because of my field of study of the Ethiopic Enoch, I would have had to go to North Africa to do research. I was not greatly disappointed in not being able to reach a Ph.D. I've never needed that, and I think the Lord was in it. But this finished my formal education.

The last visit I had with Dr. Goodspeed before leaving the University, we walked across the quadrangle. He called me by name and asked me to walk with him. At the University of Chicago you would never go up and walk with a professor unless you were invited. He invited me to join him. He said, "You're going to be graduating tomorrow. Frankly, I'm glad we send out someone like you once in awhile. I think it's good for this school." I said, "I'm not sure I know how you mean that." He said, "Well, as you know, we send out a lot of liberals into the ministry. We can't be too proud of the results they get in the ministry. I would say it is good for us to send out once in awhile someone who has your convictions." He said, "There is no doubt in my mind that you will have a very useful ministry."

He was an honest man. The reason he as a liberal was more mild was because he was saturated with this Book. For instance, we think of John 3:16 in English, and he would be thinking of it in Greek. In a class we would be discussing, perhaps, the case of extreme doubt, and he could tell you where the two operatives were in the New Testament. He could tell you the construction. His mind and heart had been so saturated with the Word of God that he just couldn't be as far out as someone would be in philosophy or someone in the field of history.

Dr. Goodspeed was supplying a large church at one time and asked me for permission to present my name to that church for the pastorate. I said, "No, Dr. Goodspeed, I'd never fit that congregation and they wouldn't fit me." He said they didn't very often get people refused that had their name presented by the University of Chicago. This was after I had graduated and was out for several months.

Chapter 5

My Life's Work

Federated Church, Wilton Center, Illinois

This brings me in my story to the time when I went out into the ministry to which I had been called.

My first church was a Federated Church between Joliet and Kankakee, Illinois, at Wilton Center. This was while I was a student at Moody Bible Institute in Chicago. I went on Friday nights for prayer meeting, and then did my visitation on Saturdays and had services on Sundays and went back to Chicago for classes on Monday mornings.

Wilton Center was a very small community with a general store at the center of town. One day in the store I was introduced to the Catholic Priest as the Baptist pastor in town. He said, "I suppose you are called a doctor. Most Baptist preachers are called doctors, which doesn't really mean much." I said, "No, I'm not a doctor, but," I said, "I suppose you are called a father. That really doesn't mean much either."

I resigned from Wilton Center Federated Church in the late summer of 1928 and moved to Kalamazoo, Michigan where I enrolled in Kalamazoo College.

First Baptist Church, Lawton, Michigan

First Baptist Church of Lawton, Michigan.

Upon arriving at Kalamazoo College, the Dean of the College, Dr. Herman Severn, took me to Lawton, Michigan to meet the Pulpit Committee of the First Baptist Church of Lawton. I was soon called to be their pastor and served there nine months while attending the college.

Bethel Baptist Church, Kalamazoo, Michigan

Bethel Baptist Church of Kalamazoo, Michigan.

After serving the Lawton Baptist Church nine months, I was called to the Bethel Baptist Church of Kalamazoo, where I served as a student pastor and later as full-time resident pastor. While serving the Bethel Baptist Church, I met Florence L. Welch, R.N., who was working for the City Health Department of Kalamazoo and married her April 17, 1935. This was part of my education, much needed and quite a little delayed! I was just a few weeks from thirty-five years of age.

I will let Mrs. Clearwaters tell in her own words our first meeting.

"I was doing public health work in Kalamazoo. We worked among the indigent at that time because of the depression. I was in a home where an elderly couple was very ill. As I went in, I was introduced to a man by a woman who had an impediment in speech. She was taking care of this elderly couple. I didn't understand just who I was meeting, so I went about my business, and the young man left. He was wearing a Chesterfield overcoat and spats and derby. I didn't think much more about it, but at noon I went back to the office, and a clerk in the office said, 'You met my pastor this morning.' I said, 'You mean a preacher?' I said, 'No, I didn't meet any preacher.' She described him, and I said, 'Well, I understood he was an insurance man.' No, she said that was her

Florence's graduation from Nurses Training as a registered nurse.

pastor. He had called her and she said, 'He wants to meet you. He wants me to arrange something so you can get together.' Then she said, 'I don't know why I should, because I like him!' But we did not get together for

Engagement, 1934.

Florence Welch 1935 Pastor's Bride

MARRIAGE TO REV. R. V. CLEARWATERS SOLEMNIZED AT STETSON CHAPEL

Stetson chapel, Kalamazoo College, was the scene of a lovely wedding at 4 Wednesday afternoon, April 17, when Miss Florence Louise Welch, daughted of Mr. and Mrs. Joseph Welch, Florence street, became the bride of the Rev. Richard V. Clearwaters, recently resigned pastor the Bethel Baptist church, son of Mr. and Mrs. Guy Clearwaters, Spokane, Wash., in a service read by the Rev. Ray E. Clearwaters, Lawton Baptist church, and brother of the bridegroom. About 300 guests were present.

The bride was attired in an off-white satin and lace gown, fashioned on train. Her white tulle veil was secured by a pearlet band, and her accessories also were white. She carried a shower bouquet of Johanna Hill roses. Miss Myrtle Bodmer, maid-of-honor, wore a pink organdie gown, and the two bridesmaids, Misses Patricia Brady and Mary Catherine Preston, appeared in blue and pink organdie, respectively, and all carried bouquets of pink roses. Dr. Harvey C. Bodmer, Kalamazoo, was best man, and ushers included Deo Kingsley, cousin of the bride, Kalamazoo, Francis Goodman, William Persons and Kendrick Nelson.

The chapel was beautifully decorated with palms and ferns, and music was presented by Burton M. Barber, pianist, and Howard Taft, vocal soloist.

After the ceremony, a reception was held in the First Baptist church parlors. The Rev. and Mrs. Clearwaters left on a motor trip to Washington, D. C., and will be at home after May 1 at 442 Fifth avenue, S. W., Cedar Rapids, Ia. The return trip from Washington will be made, via Canada. For travelling, Mrs. Clearwaters wore a blue wool ensemble, trimmed with grey wolf, and matching accessories.

Mrs. Clearwaters was graduated from Central high school and St. Camillus Training school, Borgess hospital. She was an employe of the city health department for three years, 1932-35. The Rev. Clearwaters received his A. B. degre from Kalamazoo College and his D. B. degree from the Northern Baptist Seminary, and his A M. degree from the University of Chicago. Hhe recently resigned as pastor of the Bethel Baptist church to accept a call to the Calvary Baptist church, Cedar Rapids, Ia. He was in the local pastorate for five years.

Out-of-town guests at the wedding were Mr. and Mrs. Clarence Brown, Paw Paw; Mr. and Mrs. Ernest Swanty, Mr. and Mrs. Edward Swanty, Hopkins, Mr. and Mrs. Jesse Dunham and George Dunham, Lawton; Mr. and Mrs. Billy Freas, Grand Rapids, Mr. and Mrs. Hugh Brown, Lawton; Mr. and Mrs. Samuel Almond, Allegan: Mr. and Mrs. W. A. Foster and Mr. and Mrs. Willard Bruner, Holland. Dr. and Mrs. C. D. Ewing, Lawton, and Mr. and Mrs. Lewis Cameron.

Photo by L. C. Robinson.
MISS FLORENCE WELCH
Miss Welch's engagement to the Rev. Richard V. Clearwaters is announced today by her parents, Mr. and Mrs. Joseph Welch, Florence street. The wedding will take place in April.

some time after that, because I had someone else. So it was two or more years later before we really got together. We were engaged for way over a year because of the depression. We couldn't afford to get married. I had a very secure job doing public health work, and he was making $25.00 a week as a student pastor. He was buying a car and commuting to the University of Chicago, so we just couldn't think of getting married."

Marriage, April 17, 1935.

Florence was very active in the church, and I was her pastor. We were married on April 17, 1935, in the college chapel of Kalamazoo College. My brother Roy officiated. He was a Baptist minister in Lawton,

Michigan at the time. I immediately resigned as pastor of Bethel Baptist Church to accept a "call" to the Calvary Baptist Church in Cedar Rapids, Iowa, which pastorate I assumed after our wedding trip to Canada.

Calvary Baptist Church, Cedar Rapids, Iowa

Calvary Baptist Church, Cedar Rapids, Iowa.

In many ways this was an important era in my life. When I finished my education, I made a covenant with the Lord that the first church offering me an open door, or a "call" to be pastor, I would take as His will. I had been recommended in three places: Long Island, New York (a man by the name of Dr. Sears was very anxious to have me come there); Bloomington, Illinois, a pastorate once held by Dr. W.B. Riley, a church of about a thousand members, a very desirable pulpit; and the third was Calvary Baptist Church of Cedar Rapids, Iowa. That was the first one that invited me to come to candidate and made the first offer. I went there.

I had three opportunities, all were open pulpits. My covenant was, "Lord, whichever one of these offers me the first open door, that's where I'll take it as your will I should go."

I believe the Lord is more anxious to lead us than we are to be led. And usually we miss the Lord's leading because we are absolutely not surrendered. If we are surrendered, we are winning souls to Christ—that's why He saved us, to serve. You're not surrendered to God when you waste your time, when you don't witness, when you are slothful and not faithful in reading your Bible and praying. God saw the folly of Israel, they wanted a king. It wasn't God's will, and I read in the Scriptures He gave them the desires of their heart. They got God's second or third best, but He sent leanness into their souls. It's my honest and convicted opinion that about two-thirds of theological students and servants in the Lord's field are getting God's second and third and fourth best.

Let me give you an instance. I was called to Chicago by a former professor of mine to supply his pulpit. He got over sixty dollars for that week, and he left an envelope for me with fifteen dollars for preaching morning and evening, teaching a Sunday School class and speaking to the young people and traveling some one hundred sixty miles round trip at my own expense. This same man was invited to join the faculty of the Western Theological Seminary, which post he was willing to accept part-time provided they could find him a place where he could preach and supplement his income. He was called to a church, but put the call in his pocket because he heard that a much larger church was opening up. So he manipulated and got himself before the large church, carrying the other call in his pocket until the large church finally voted to call him. At that time he felt called to the large church and didn't feel called to teach in the seminary any more. Do I need to tell you this is in the flesh? Do I need to tell you God's hand of blessing is never on this kind of thing? Do I need to tell you it only brings misery?

I think people that operate this way, their GPC degree is not "Go Preach Christ", but rather "Go Plow Corn". I think the ministry would be better off if such men never opened the Bible, never stood before a people, if there is nothing they have to depend on—no leading of the Lord.

Many students have to decide what they are going to do, and begin shaping everything toward that goal and end up in a big fizzle. God says, "I have formed thee; I knew thee." The "I" is God. But many students shape their own lives, and if they accomplish it, I think it'll leave not much room for the Lord.

There are so many people going around deciding what they're going to do and how they're going to do it, and then find peers that will tell them that's the way to do it. The blind lead the blind, and all fall in the ditch. My life's verse is Phil. 1:21, and my advice is, you better let the Lord shape your course. You better ask Him and commit to Him, and you will always be grateful.

Cedar Rapids was the first offer. The church had a six thousand dollar mortgage on a wooden-frame building for which the wrecking company had offered them five hundred dollars. They wanted us to come for fifteen hundred dollars per year and parsonage. I laid my financial obligation before them and stated that I could not make both ends meet on that salary, and they raised it to eighteen hundred and parsonage.

They did not believe in giving by envelope. It had been served about five years by a man who was an evangelist in his own right, but he was mostly an exhorter—there were a lot of untrained Christians. I said I would come if they would give me a signed-up statement of the storehouse tithers in the church. That was with my acceptance. In four and one-half years we paid off the mortgage and had ten thousand dollars in a building fund.

Going to the Calvary Baptist Church in Cedar Rapids, Iowa, was a very fortunate thing. I had only been out of school a little while. I went to a purely industrial people. They loved the Word of God and they loved souls. We were just immersed there, my wife and I, for four and a half years, in the ministry of preaching the Gospel and evangelism. The first two or three years we were there I held my own evangelistic meetings, and we would have yearly a hundred and fifty people forward in response to the invitation. I have tried to remember, but I don't believe at that time in the church there would have been more than three college graduates. But it was God's place for me. These members were very evangelistic and fundamental, and during the 1936 severe winter the weekly calling night for members averaged between thirty-five and forty each week when the temperature was hovering between thirty and forty degrees below zero.

While serving in Cedar Rapids, I was elected President of the Iowa Baptist State Convention. This gave me personal acquaintance and contact with the national leaders of the American Baptist Convention and also with other State leaders.

Fourth Baptist Church, Minneapolis, Minnesota

Fourth Baptist Church in 1922.

Fourth Baptist Church original sanctuary.

Fourth Baptist Church.

Late in the year 1939 we were visited by the Pulpit Committee of the Fourth Baptist Church of Minneapolis, Minnesota, and after a visit to the church we were extended a "call". What triggered the positive decision was that we had seen the mortgage in Cedar Rapids paid off, and the small building was full to capacity morning and evening with souls being saved regularly and a sizeable sum in a building fund. After two meetings the Advisory Board of the church refused to make any decision about going ahead with plans to build.

At that time I recommended two men for Fourth Baptist Church instead of considering it myself, but they wrote back and said they didn't want my recommendations; they wanted me to come to candidate. When I came there was no question in my mind that God wanted me there. On the way back to Cedar Rapids my wife and I were riding along, and we hadn't said anything for quite awhile. You know how it goes sometimes. Then she said, "What are you thinking about?" There's only one person in the world who can ask you what you are thinking about, and that's your wife. And she may not always find out! "I was just thinking that when you get back to Cedar Rapids you better start taking the curtains down. We're going to Minneapolis." She said, "You better wait until they do some voting." Wives have a way of keeping you humble! I said, "The Lord spoke to me last night." I have never had a question, but that this is where the Lord wanted me. On the way up I had little interest in the place. But I knew it made no difference what the vote was. There were fifty-two negative votes when I came to the Fourth Baptist Church, but that didn't make a bit of difference. If it had been a majority of one, I would have come because I got the call from the Lord and it was ratified by the people (the theocracy—we're under shepherds of the Lord, and the democracy—the Lord's leading ratified by the people, at work). I was on the field January 1, 1940.

Clearwaters family in 1941, Richard, Jane and Florence.

Clearwaters family 1949.

Clearwaters family 1980.

Tenth anniversary at Fourth Baptist Church.

Fifteenth anniversary at Fourth Baptist Church.

Ground breaking in 1972 for new sanctuary.

Richard V. Clearwaters ground breaking in 1962 for gym.

Fourth Baptist Church as it stands today.

Dr. Richard V. Clearwaters with former youth pastors. Dr. Earl Matteson, far left; Dr. Richard V. Clearwaters, Rev. Donald Nelson, Rev. Paul Fosmark.

40th anniversary at Fourth Baptist Church, 1980.

New sanctuary, 1980.

40th anniversary at Fourth Baptist Church, 1980.

40th anniversary at Fourth Baptist Church, 1980.

Fourth Baptist Church was organized in 1881 and established on its present site in 1918. Nine pastors served the church over more than the one hundred years of existence. The church historian writes, "It was under Dr. Richard V. Clearwaters' ministry, beginning in 1940 and continuing for some forty-two years, that the church enjoyed a widening scope of influence and significant patterns of growth."

By May of 1940 a new Bible school fire-proof building, 40 feet wide by 80 feet long and three floors was dedicated. This helped to make room for a growing Sunday School that was using overflow space in a funeral chapel nearby and a theater on Broadway for two large Sunday School classes.

The ministry here has been a series of miracles. So many things have happened, some of it because of people and some of it in spite of people. The Lord has marched on as though some irresistible force had been carrying a banner and whatever way the breezes were blowing, it made no difference. I am sure that nobody could possibly have arranged the series of events.

Conservative Baptist Association

When I accepted the pastorate of the Fourth Baptist Church, the church was a member of the Minnesota Baptist Association which was at that time an adjunct of the Northern Baptist Convention, later to become the American Baptist Convention. It was committed to the INCLUSIVE POLICY. This term means that both fundamentalists and liberals were welcome in this fellowship and its leadership. The principles of the Inclusive Policy were diametrically opposed to the Biblical principle of separation. For a time there seemed to be no sharp issue raised over this unbiblical mixture, but as time went on certain groups, such as the General Association of Regular Baptists, withdrew from the liberal convention, and the remaining members were dominated by liberals, who grew so bold that they began to invite the fundamentalists to get out and leave.

By this time a group of fundamentalists had organized a "Fundamental Fellowship" within the American Baptist Convention. The early leaders of this group were Jasper Cortentus Massee, James Whitcomb Brougher, W.B. Riley, Earle V. Pierce, and others. These leaders had no intention of separating from the liberal convention, so the convicted separatist members gradually withdrew. In the case of the Minnesota Baptist Convention in 1948, after the Northern Baptist Convention met in Grand Rapids, Michigan, the Minnesota Convention withdrew as an organization. The Fourth Baptist Church and I as its pastor was in this group.

> "The struggle for a fundamentalist state convention in Minnesota was a long and painful battle. The Minnesota Baptist Convention had submitted itself to the Northern Convention's machinery in hope that it would result in a greater effort to spread the Gospel in Minnesota. But with the financial support, the Northern Convention's leadership demanded absolute loyalty to all of their agencies regardless of the doctrinal implications.
>
> "Under the leadership of William B. Riley, the Minnesota Baptist Convention refused to accept the demands of the national leadership of their liberal-oriented program. But there were some in Minnesota who knew that opposition by itself was not the answer. One of these was Dr. Richard V. Clearwaters, pastor of the Fourth Baptist Church of Minneapolis. Within a year after the funda-

> mentalist victory in 1946, Dr. Clearwaters was already designing a new national organization that would not tolerate either liberalism or modernism. It was he who led the Minnesota Baptist Convention from a fundamentalist to a separatistic organization."[1]

When the Conservative Baptist movement was breaking away from the American Baptist Convention, the big issue was the matter of the virgin birth of Christ. Those who believed in it were included in the program with those who didn't believe in it, and they were appointed as missionaries and leaders. The Northern Baptist Convention had adopted the inclusive policy with its deficiency in devotion to the Word of God and divergent views of the doctrines of this Book. We as a fundamentalist Board met with their Board, and I was asked to represent our Board. At one session on one side of the table were the leaders of the Conservative Baptists and on the other side were the leaders of the foreign mission society of the Convention. I was asked to lead off the discussion. I said, "I would like to read a passage from Luke's gospel." Then I read Luke 1:35, "And the angel answered and said unto her, The Holy Ghost shall come upon thee, and the power of the Highest shall overshadow thee; therefore, also that holy thing which shall be born of thee shall be called the Son of God." Then I read Matthew 1:20: "But while he thought on these things, behold, the angel of the Lord appeared unto him in a dream, saying, Joseph, thou son of David, fear not to take unto thee Mary thy wife: for that which is conceived in her is of the Holy Ghost." I said, "I've read the only authority I know for the virgin birth. Matthew gives us one genealogy of the parents and Luke another. The only way to establish the paternity of a child is the testimony of the father and the mother. The Bible gives us both. I want to know if you gentlemen receive and accept this authority." Well, they said, not unless we interpret it. I said, "Well, in a court of law, all language is accepted as it is in common usage. This is a document, and when documents are presented in court, they are accepted in the language of common usage. All of these words are very simple. Do you accept them in the language of common usage?" They didn't of course. They rejected the Word of God. They immediately revealed they were not submitting their minds on the virgin birth. We

1. Becklund, David, *History of the Minnesota Baptist Convention*, (1967), pp. 57-58.

have no other place to go for our authority. At that point, I exercised my principle of being a Biblicist. Do you accept the Word of God on the subject of the virgin birth? No, they said, unless we interpret it. It meant they were going to put their own ideas on the revealed Word of God.

That was a very strategic moment, and I lost a lot of friends. They didn't think I was very broadminded! I said I'm just as broadminded as the Bible is and just as narrow-minded as the Bible.

In 1943 in Chicago I convened the first section of the Conservative Baptist Association of America. Later the eastern section of the country did the same, and later again the West Section; and the National Conservative Baptist Association of America was organized. I served as President of this organization for three years. It totaled about twelve hundred to fifteen hundred member churches, and Dr. B. Myron Cedarholm served as the Executive Secretary for eighteen years.

From 1943 to 1963 during the organization and growth of the

Conservative Baptist movement, I was called upon as an expert witness in various courts in which the American Baptist Convention served an injunction against local churches, claiming the local Baptist church property for themselves because the churches had left the American Baptist Convention. When conventionism was rampant in the American Baptist Convention, some local Baptist churches in the Chicago Association could negotiate a large collateral bank loan, using the local church property as security for the loan. I know of no other Association that did this.

The routine in these court cases, none of which were successful in stealing the local church property from the church, was very simple. As defendants, we usually asked the Convention to show their "legal title", which of course they could not. After this junction in the procedure, we produced *The Year Book of the Northern Baptist Convention*, which printed in every annual yearbook this DECLARATION as an act to incorporate, which read:

> "The Northern Baptist Convention declares its belief in the independence of the local church, and in the purely advisory nature of all denominational organizations composed of representatives of churches. It believes also that in view of the growth of the Baptist denomination, and its extension throughout our country there is need for an organization to serve the common interests of the entire denomination as state and district organizations serve their respective constituents."

Thus, they declared in their legal incorporation their "belief in the independence of the local church, and in the purely advisory nature of all denominational organizations". And it believes also that "there is need for an organization to serve the common interests of the entire denomination, as state and district organizations serve their respective constituents".

The self-declared convictions of the Northern Baptist Convention disqualified them in court to claim property of a local Baptist church: independence of the local Baptist church, the purely advisory nature of all denominational organizations, the national organization is purposed to serve the churches—not control, and the national organization is purposed to serve the local church as the State organization served.

But with all of these self-declared disqualifications, the Northern Baptist Convention repeatedly tried to steal local Baptist church property and failed in Algona, Iowa; Fort Collins, Colorado; Waupaca, Wisconsin; Richfield, Minnesota; and Bloomington, Illinois. All of these experiences were occasions which provided a setting for Baptists to learn more about their historic Baptist principles, and to learn from history that Baptists through the centuries had been persecuted for these principles, but at no time in Baptist history that the Baptists had ever been persecutors of others for their religious faith.

These various litigations were "petitions in equity" to settle the dispute of ownership of property before a judge, without a jury. On one occasion I recall after the judge decided for us, the defendants, one of the high officials of the Northern Baptist Convention made this remark, "If we should have had a Roman Catholic judge, we no doubt would have won our case, because they have more respect for a large ecclesiastical organization than a Protestant judge." It would not have altered the decision, however, because such decisions are decided on supporting evidence on points of law, not on the personal view or conviction of the judge presiding on the bench.

When the Conservative Baptist Association became twenty years old, it was practicing the inclusive policy that we protested in the American Baptist Convention. After the 1963 Conservative Baptist Convention in California, I withdrew from them.

Central Baptist Theological Seminary

As a trustee of the Northwestern Theological Seminary, I voted against that seminary being discontinued, and I also opposed the dropping of the Northwestern Bible College. Both schools were dropped in favor of one school, Northwestern College, instead of trying to operate three schools.

At the behest of a large deputation who waited upon me, I organized the Central Baptist Theological Seminary in 1956 with thirty-one students. The professors the first year got two cents a mile for their cars and no salary. I quote from the Central Baptist Theological Seminary Catalog of 1984-1986, page 6:

Richard V. Clearwaters, President, Central Theological Seminary.

"When the Northwestern Theological Seminary, begun by Dr. William Bell Riley, was discontinued after over twenty years, there remained a vacuum in the Minneapolis area. Both students and faculty urged Dr. Richard V. Clearwaters to spearhead establishment of a fundamental Baptist theological seminary. President Richard Elvee of Northwestern College wrote, 'In order that there may be no misunderstanding among all of our friends, I would like to say that this investigation of the possibilities for founding a conservative Baptist seminary on the part of Richard V. Clearwaters is being carried on with my full knowledge and consent. The dropping of the seminary of Northwestern College was a decision on the part of the Board of Directors necessitated by our financial inability to carry on three schools.' To house the new school, the Fourth Baptist Church kindly, graciously, and unanimously agreed to provide its commodious and spacious premises for the housing

First Seminary faculty.

> of the school, the only expense the Seminary to bear being such services as the church would not furnish in serving itself. Thus Central Seminary began with a full three-year schedule on September 11, 1956. That fall thirty-one students from ten states began studying under a faculty of seven. Approval for veterans' training was granted by the Minnesota State Board of Education within two months, retroactive to the opening of school.
>
> "Within seven years Central Seminary had grown to a student body of over one hundred students, enjoying enlarged housing in the expanded facilities of Fourth Baptist Church, engaging in a printing and radio ministry in addition to classroom and Bible conference work. Central graduates serve in various states of the United States and on many foreign mission fields."

Central Seminary is a graduate school of learning. The standard seminary degree (Master of Divinity) requires four years of college and three years of seminary residence work. Post-graduate degrees are also offered. In addition, the Seminary has programs leading to a diploma in Bible and Theology and Christian Education. The Seminary stationery has always carried the dictum, "When the Lord calls to preach, He calls to prepare."

> Central Seminary since its beginning in 1956 has maintained a set of distinctives outlined by Dr. Clearwaters in the Points of Purpose carried in every catalog. Among these are: the direct method of presenting truth from the Bible; an emphasis on "scholarship of the highest order"; local church in ideology; Baptistic, not interdenominational; dispensational, not covenant reformed in theology; pretribulational in eschatology; separatistic, not ecumenical. The seminary emphasizes evangelism, preaching and missions, being known for its "balance" between high academics and genuine concern for others. The core of the curriculum is correct theology and careful Biblical exegesis.[1]

Pillsbury Baptist Bible College

Pillsbury Baptist Bible College of Owatonna, Minnesota, was organized in 1957. The Pillsbury Baptist Bible College Catalog for

1. Fourth Baptist Church Centennial Book (1981), "Central Seminary".

1982-1984, page 21, gives this summary of the history of Pillsbury College:

> "Minnesota Central University was granted a charter by the Minnesota Legislature on March 4, 1854, and was operated at Hastings, Minnesota, until 1868 when it closed due to financial and other difficulties. However, the Minnesota Baptist State Convention again felt the need for a Baptist college, and on September 10, 1877, opened the Minnesota Academy at Owatonna, Minnesota, continuing securities and other properties of Minnesota Central University. The name of the school was changed to Pillsbury Academy in 1886 in honor of one of its chief donors, the honorable George A. Pillsbury of the First Baptist Church, Minneapolis, and one-time mayor of the city. A strong Baptist university was intended, but only the academy materialized.
>
> "Sponsored by Mr. Pillsbury, a boarding hall for women was erected in 1886 and later Old Main for administration and classrooms, the music hall, the drill hall, and the central heating plant. Kelly Hall was dedicated in 1904 as a men's dormitory. It was destroyed by fire in February 1939. The name Kelly was then transferred to the present music building—Kelly Hall. In 1911 Jefts Hall was erected as a dining commons, and in 1914 Lindsay Hall was built to house the gymnasium and swimming pool."

Pillsbury College.

Pillsbury College.

Pillsbury College Homecoming.

Dr. Richard V. Clearwaters and Dr. Joseph Rammel.

Pillsbury Baptist Bible College was for many years an academy controlled by theological liberals. In 1920 it became a military academy for boys only. Though there were some principles of discipline and character building taught at Pillsbury in those days, the purpose of the Academy was far removed from its original purpose of training men and women for Christian service.

> Through the efforts primarily of Dr. Clearwaters, the school began to move back towards a Biblicist position. Eventually the Minnesota Supreme Court ruled that the Minnesota Baptist Association had the right to choose the trustees to the Academy. Thus in 1957 Pillsbury opened its doors as a fundamentalist Baptist Bible College. Dr. Clearwaters was the first president.
>
> Perhaps no one person has had as much influence in the shaping of the philosophy, theology, and direction of Pillsbury Baptist Bible College as Dr. Clearwaters. Dr. Clearwaters was the key man in the battle to take Pillsbury out of the hands of the theological liberals. He led in the change of Pillsbury Academy to Pillsbury Baptist Bible College, served as the college's first President, was the

Dr. Richard V. Clearwaters and Dr. Joseph Rammel.

Former presidents of Pillsbury College left to right: Dr. Richard V. Clearwaters, Dr. Monroe Parker, Dr. B. Myron Cedarholm, Dr. Joseph Rammel.

> Chairman of the Board of Trustees, and later guided the college as President once again during an hour of crisis. Dr. Clearwaters continues to serve sacrificially on the Board of Trustees of Pillsbury, as well as President Emeritus. Today Pillsbury has grown to well over 700 students, with an outstanding faculty, and godly president in Dr. Joseph Rammel. Thus, the impact of Dr. Clearwaters' interest in education will be felt for years to come in the lives of hundreds of young men and women.[1]

Today the current president of Pillsbury Baptist Bible College, Dr. Allen Potter, is a product of the youth program of the Fourth Baptist Church, is a graduate of Pillsbury Baptist Bible College, and a graduate of Central Seminary. I was bestowed the honor of President Emeritus of Pillsbury College in 1975.

Fourth Baptist Bible Institute

In 1958 we organized the Monday evening Bible Institute in the church. It's the same grade of education one can get at Pillsbury College.

> Fourth Baptist Bible Institute was founded in 1958 in accord with the vision of our pastor, Dr. Clearwaters, for systematic Bible study for lay Christian men and women. The initial year began with 110 students and six faculty members. The institute has grown substantially since then, but its aims and purposes have remained unchanged.
>
> The institute aims to provide a thorough Bible knowledge coupled with training in specific areas of practical ministry. Such training is not to be viewed as an end in itself, but rather, all the training is designed to equip the believer for mature and effective service to his or her local church.[2]

Camp Clear-Waters

A family by the name of Peterson owned 320 acres of land on the St. Croix River, about thirty miles from us as the crow flies, and they were after me for two years to have the church buy the 320 acres. I kept putting them off, and the third year they called me up, and they said if

---

1. Fourth Baptist Church Centennial Book (1981), "Pillsbury Baptist Bible College."
2. Fourth Baptist Church Centennial Book (1981), "Fourth Baptist Bible Institute".

you don't want the land by this weekend, on Monday they would put it on the market. They offered the 320 acres for $15,000.00. We were in the process of a big building program. The church didn't have a dollar.

Don Nelson was the youth pastor. We would not have the camp if it had not been for Don Nelson. We had a nationally-known youth program then. When we went to the annual meetings in Portland, Don assembled five hundred people on a Saturday afternoon in a meeting to present the youth program at Fourth Baptist Church. Everybody in the nation knew of the Fourth Baptist youth program.

Don got a couple of buses of men to go out to look at the acreage on a Sunday afternoon. And so when they got back, they were all pushing for this land. It went through unanimously, and we had a trustee meeting, and the first thing they asked me, "Well, Doc, how are you going to pay for it?" We needed $15,000.00 cash. "Well," I said, "On Thursday night I'll get up and announce that we'll pay $1500.00 a year for ten years." We got a mortgage on our parsonage, which was clear then, and we got the cash and gave it to them. We had fifty people give $30.00 a year. That's the way we paid for it, and nobody knew we were paying it.

> On January 31, 1963, the youth of the Fourth Baptist Church voted unanimously to name the camp in honor of their pastor, Dr. Richard V. Clearwaters, who loves youth and is loved by them. This request was then unanimously ratified by the church at a Sunday evening service, February 3, 1963.[1]

The church at that time was in a whole new building program. There was no way we could do anything in the way of building, and the people had to understand that we were not going to build anything in that area until we got the land paid for. Don Nelson said we'll have a wilderness camp. We won't build anything out there. However, we did make a master plan for building on the land, the drainage and all the rest of it was selected, so later when the lodge was built, it got placed exactly where the master plan said it had to go. In 1967 a year-round facility, seating around 200 people and able to feed about that many in the dining room, was built with much volunteer help from the church. It is still one

1. Fourth Baptist Church Centennial Book (1981), "Camp Clear-Waters".

Dr. Richard V. Clearwaters on horse at Camp Clear-Waters.

Lodge at Camp Clear-Waters.

of the outstanding camps in the country.

WCTS-FM — The Bible Station

One morning I had a man from a very well known large radio corporation here in town call me up. He wanted to take me to lunch. He told me about property for sale. He said, "I heard you had some interest in a radio station." He just led me into it. I had been praying for a radio station that would honor the Lord in every way, and I felt this was the beginning of the answer to my prayers. That's how we got the Jones Lake property at a very nominal sum. This property was suited to radio towers, and so plans were set in operation in search for a frequency on which we might broadcast.

In those years FM broadcasting was beginning, because most of us didn't have those kinds of radios. They weren't making AM-FM sets at that time. We furnished FM radios to folks for a gift to the station.

First WCTS studio.

There was a Free Church in town that had an FM station, and they lost it and sold out, a really sacrificial sale. For $25,000.00 they sold everything they had acquired. When they went on the air, they estimated there were not over 50,000 FM sets in the city. Our frequency came to us as 100.3, and we called it The Bible Station and took Psalm 100:3 as our verse.

I remember when we got permission to broadcast. My wife and I and Jane were at the stadium watching a Twins ball game. And it came over the loudspeaker that Dr. Clearwaters was wanted at the office. It was rather shocking. We thought something terrible had happened. It was Neal Kemp who had gotten on the phone, and he thought the news was so good it couldn't wait. He called to say we had gotten permission to broadcast. Later we said, "How did anyone know we were out here?" It shows that we have to be careful because people know where we are all the time." Everybody in the whole stadium knew we were there, and so for a week or more the people said, "I heard you were at the ball game."

When we started broadcasting, people thought we were foolish. I didn't know beans about radio or electronics, and I knew it. Chuck Alderson put his knowledge behind what we wanted to do and spent many hours working at it. The Bible Station has increased in power through the years and now reaches a much larger area with twenty-four hours of broadcasting the gospel and Christ-honoring music.

Retirement

I never had any doubt that the Lord would let me know when my ministry is through. In December of 1981, God led me to resign. After my retirement, the church voted to confer upon me the honorary title of Pastor Emeritus.

A large radio and television syndicate from Omaha, Nebraska, was constructing a new 1644-foot tower near Anoka and invited WCTS-FM as the only other station to share the tower with them, it being the tallest tower in the surrounding five-state area. Because of this venture, the Trustees asked me to continue as President of the Seminary until the completion and operation of the tower. I continued also as a part-time professor in the Seminary. After my retirement, the Trustees honored

Retirement from Central Theological Seminary in 1986.

Retirement from Fourth Baptist Church, 1982.

me with the title of President Emeritus of the Seminary.

And so, we have now five great buildings here at Fourth Baptist, and there is no place in the junction of my ministry that I can't immediately say that I was only an instrument. I wasn't a causitive instrument—I was only an instrument in the hand of God. That's what you ought to be, an instrument yielded to His grasp. If you're not, you'll not accomplish the most for Him.

To love someone more dearly every day,
To help some wandering child to find his way,
To ponder over a noble thought and pray,
And smile when evening falls,
This is my task.

Then My Saviour by and by to meet,
When faith hath made her task on earth complete,
And lay my trophy at the Master's feet,
Within the jasper walls,
This crowns my task.

(**My Task**. Words taken from "Lorenz's Gospel Soloist", copyright 1939 by the Lorenz Publishing Co., used by permission.)

Historic Dates in the Progress of the Fourth Baptist Church

History

1881—December 19 organized building formerly known as Jewett Chapel, 11th Avenue North and Lyndale
1885—New Building erected at 18th and Dupont
1915—Property purchased, 2105 Fremont Avenue North
1919—Basement completed and occupied
1922—Church dedicated, November 5
1940—Dr. R.V. Clearwaters became pastor
1940—Dedicated Bible School building
1956—Central Baptist Seminary organized
1956—Central Baptist Seminary Press
1957—Pillsbury Baptist Bible College started

1958—September—Fourth Baptist Bible Institute was organized
1962—Annex building and gymnasium built
1963—Camp purchased in Wisconsin on the St. Croix
1965—The license for WCTS-FM (The Bible Station) was granted to Central Seminary, June 26
1966—Fourth Baptist Christian Day School organized in the fall with kindergarten through fourth grade (60 students)
1968—Lodge built at Camp Clear-Waters; Dedicated May 30
1970—Fourth Baptist Christian Day School and Sunday School building built
1973—2400 capacity church auditorium built
1982—Dr. R.V. Clearwaters retired

Fourth Baptist Church is a complex of five large buildings, the home of:

Central Baptist Theological Seminary of Minneapolis, founded in 1956.

Fourth Baptist Bible Institute, founded in 1958.

Fourth Baptist Sunday School and Youth Groups, using the Bible as a textbook, and housed in quarters including a gymnasium, with a full standard-sized playing floor with modern showers and locker rooms, built in 1962-63.

WCTS-FM radio, 100.3 on the FM dial, of Central Baptist Theological Seminary, broadcasting twenty-four hours a day, with studios located in the church building, established in 1965.

Fourth Baptist Christian Day School, K through 12 in 1973, established in 1966.

Fourth Baptist Wilderness Youth Camp located on hundreds of acres of native woodland, thirty miles away on the beautiful St. Croix River with a new $50,000.00 lodge for summer and winter use, built in 1967.

Fourth Baptist Sunday School and Christian Day School building, built in 1970.

Fourth Baptist auditorium, 2400 capacity, with adequate parking, built in 1973.

CHAPTER 6

A Self-Declared Biblicist

A Biblicist is one who accepts the Bible as Jesus defined it. ". . . one jot or one tittle shall in no wise pass from the law till all be fulfilled." Matt. 5:18.

> "All Scripture is given by inspiration of God, and is profitable for doctrine, for reproof, for correction, for instruction in righteousness." II Tim. 3:16

It's 50% useful in positive matters and 50% useful in negative matters, a full-orbed body of truth. To become Biblicists we have to take a position of separation and find that there is nothing, nobody, no individual can separate us from the Word of God. Nothing can come between us and the Bible, nothing between us and the Lord, and nothing between us and our fellowman. Those three tenets are all violated by the general concept of the Catholic Church, a man-made organization and a man-controlled organization, and therefore cannot be relied upon as having divine authority.

We come then to the first step. That means that *all* of the Bible is important. Jesus referred to even jots and tittles. We cannot say this part is important in the Bible and this part isn't important. If we were to remove some part of the Bible at some time and place, it will be missed.

W.B. Riley, long time friend, counselor and mentor.

I was thinking of the passage of Scripture in II Tim. 4:13 where Paul asked Timothy when you come bring my coat which I left at Troas. Suppose we say it is not important that Paul asked for his coat. One time Vernon Grounds called us literalists and worshipping a black book, etc., and said, "Who on earth would ever say that the Bible talking about Paul wanting his coat would ever say that was important." I had never thought of that before and I read it over. "The cloke that I left at Troas with Carpus, when thou comest, bring with thee, and the books, but especially the parchments." Now, supposing we say it's not important that Paul asked for his cloke. Well, that was a physical need he had, the books—of human origin—was a mental need, but especially the parchments, which were the divine authority, was a spiritual need he had. It isn't an accident that it was put that way. You can't say it wasn't important that Paul wanted his coat. It fits in the setting, and you violate the text and context if you don't keep it in that order. Look at the order you have: physical, mental and spiritual. Paul had perfect order. Misplaced priorities are one of the biggest sins we have today. Paul was producing an order of priorities. So every jot and tittle is important. The whole Bible is important.

II Cor. 2:17, "For we are not as many, which corrupt the Word of God, but as of sincerity, but as of God, in the sight of God speak we in Christ." Words are used to communicate knowledge, and the Bible uses words. I Cor. 2:13, "Which things also we speak, not in the words which man's wisdom teacheth, but which the Holy Ghost teacheth; comparing spiritual things with spiritual." Every word is important. A Biblicist will appeal to the words and all of the words of Scripture.

The ordinances of the church are as much a part of the warp and woof of the New Testament as the historical facts. For example, the Reformers derived things from the Bible which the Bible doesn't teach. They derived infant baptism because it was easier to accept the tradition and the teaching of the Catholic Church than it was to take a stand for baptismal confession of faith in believer's baptism. When you refuse believer's baptism, you automatically deny the doctrine of separation. A church then takes unregenerates into the membership, even though they are children, who may grow up without an experience with God. They only hope and pray that they will sometime be regenerated, but many of them never are. Consequently they have saved and unsaved in the membership. This violates the Word of God. Infant baptism in itself is a denial of separation. This is why in some infant-baptizing churches they confuse Christian education with the matter of regeneration. Back in the days of the American Sunday School Union Christian education was defined in a way that was broad enough to accept the infant-baptizing churches and also those who believe in a regenerated church membership. They called it a process of nurture. Now the Bible says, "Ye must be born again." It's not a process. And it's not nurture. It's an act. A process of nurture is an entirely different expression from anything you find on becoming a Christian in the Word of God. You have to deny everything but believer's baptism by immersion to have a separated body of believers. You have to begin with the Bible teaching on the subject.

On the matter of communion, many of these infant-baptizing churches believe that you enter Christ by infant baptism and Christ enters you by the communion wafer. Nothing could be farther from the truth. These are derived things from the Bible, which the Bible doesn't teach, all tangled together and occur when they don't follow the ordinances as they are written. And notice the abuse that has been made of it. We hear of these great conventions of unseparated believers, with a great symbol of unity, all having the Lord's supper together. It is served to the saved and the unsaved alike.

The ordinances of the church are just as much a part of the whole Word of God. If you violate one part, you violate it all. It's all a solid unit put together. So I think a Biblicist gets to be a lonely person first of all because he is called a "literalist" or a "worshipper of a black book". He believes the whole Bible is inspired, every word and every jot and tittle, not in words which man's wisdom teacheth, but which the Holy Ghost teacheth, comparing spiritual things with spiritual.

Many translators do violence to the Word of God. For instance, "Through the blood of His cross" Phillips omits the word "blood", so that it reads, "Sacrifice of the cross".

These self-styled translators are diluting (polluting might be a better term) the Bible by twisting it to accommodate their updated theology. I remember in 1946 there was a crisis in the Northern Baptist Convention in Grand Rapids, and I walked into Carl Henry's office. He was then teaching in Northern Seminary. It was just before the Convention. "My," he said, "what's going to happen in Grand Rapids? What do you think it looks like?" "Well," I said, "it looks like an accident going somewhere to happen." There was a great conflict between the fundamentalists and the modernists. "Well," he said, "However it comes out," (remember this was in 1946; it's been quite a while since 1946, some decades in there. I remember it as well as yesterday.) "Well," he said, "I'll tell you, Dick, we might just as well face it. What we conservatives are going to have to do is to re-write all of the textbooks to update them, to match the scientific age in which we live."

A generation ago Colonel Robert G. Ingersoll went around the country as an infidel and challenged Bible believers, but people knew he was an infidel. He did not make any bones about it; he was not an imposter. He was not a hypocrite playing the role of someone he was not. They knew when he came to town he believed in no God when he would hold out his hand holding his watch, saying, "If there is a God in heaven, let him strike me dead in a minute." Of course, he waited, and one brother said, "I wonder if the gentleman thinks he can exhaust God's patience in one minute." A little Scotchman once answered back when Ingersoll was challenging him (Ingersoll didn't like anyone to talk back to him), and Ingersoll said to him, "If I were down there, I could swallow you in one bite." The little Scotchman said, "If you did, you'd have more brains in your stomach than you got in your head." By the way, one time Ingersoll was in Chicago (he was in D.L. Moody's day, you know) he ran for Governor of Illinois. He didn't make it. He was on a tram car, and an argument was going on between this man, Ingersoll (he was very provacative) and another man. Pretty soon a dear old lady spoke up in defense of the man who was standing for the Word of God, and Ingersoll said, "Lady, I admire your sincerity, but tell me one thing your God ever did." Well," she said, "He kept Colonel Robert G. Ingersoll from being Governor of Illinois."

The Biblicist also has to have a theology. This is a sad situation today. Many times we have people who will be in the same body of believers, some believing they can get their salvation and lose it. We have inroads today of Pentecostalism in Protestant and Catholic schools and churches which have never been known before. The reason is because they do not have a Biblical theology. The first Dean of Central Baptist Theological Seminary said the best pamphlet that ever came from my pen was "The Bible, Its Own Interpreter". That's been in print a long time, and I've never heard any respectable criticism of it. The outline of it is just as good today as it was when I wrote it. The Bible is its own interpreter. Theology means the science of God. It means the scientific use of God's book, the authority of the Word of God.

When you reduce Christianity to a philosophy, it takes its place among the philosophies of the world, and even though you may call it the queen of the philosophies, Christianity was never intended to be a philosophy.

Gradualism has afflicted the whole world. Like old Stalin said in 1932, "We're performing a great experience," he said, "in Communist Russia of peaceful co-existence with the non-Communist nations."

Peaceful co-existence was picked up by all of the religions of the world until it is now sinful to defend anything. It's picked up by the various denominations. Distinctions are wrong. Why? Think of this progression: What is a backslider? A backslider is one who is giving less and less attention to this Book. He is one who is deficient in his devotion to the Word of God. What is a heretic? This is the way gradualism leads. A heretic is one who has defections in doctrine because of his lack of devotion to the Word. But what's the third step? The third step is denial of the truth. That makes him an apostate.

The Westminster Confession of Faith believed in the Word of God as the absolute rule of faith and practice, but they didn't want so much devotion to the Word of God, so what did they do? They eliminated that phrase and they said, "Jesus Christ is our absolute rule of faith and practice." It was made easy to have less devotion to the Word of God. Gradualism—man wants more and more of sin until it delivers him in hell, and a born-again Christian wants more and more of the Word until it delivers him in heaven. Gradualism has no place to turn around. Gradualism begins in a deficiency in devotion to the Word. It's pretty hard to fight a Biblicist. They're fighting this Book. You can't fight the Word without revealing yourself, that you're on the side of the Devil.

In 1943 when we started the Conservative Baptist Mission Society, the American Foreign Mission Society adopted what was called the inclusive policy. In the inclusive policy they treated them all alike, if they supported the program of the Convention. Maybe they believed in the virgin birth and they might not. They might believe in the absolute authority of the Word of God, and they might not. But if they supported the program, they were received. That was the inclusive policy. Let me tell you where the inclusive policy leads. For example, A.J. Gordon established a seminary out in the East. For historic purposes I went to his little church where he founded the seminary just to see what it was like. There was a student ministering there to about forty people. The old Gay '90 furniture still there, the old faded seat pads. It was a Baptist church and he established a Baptist Seminary. What happened? The New England Evangelical Association, headed by Wesley Huber and John W. Granberry, Editor of the Watchman Examiner, an international Baptist paper, were both trustees of the seminary. One of them made the motion and the other supported it that Gordon Seminary cease to be

Baptist, and it became an interdenominational school. It unanimously passed. You see, interdenominationalism is a large field where people with divergent beliefs in the doctrines of the Bible can get together and be under the same umbrella. Principles of interdenominationalism: deficiency in devotion to the Word of God and divergent views of the doctrines of this Book.

G. Campbell Morgan said, "An evangelical is one who believes that all men are lost on the one hand, and on the other hand he believes that Christ came to save them." They don't define the lostness in Bible terms and they don't define salvation in Bible terms. That's why we can all hide under the umbrella. It's a big rubber word, "Evangelical".

A Biblicist is a literalist. The basis of teaching a Biblical theology in a school or seminary is really a strong emphasis on the Bible. But it has to be in the confines of a local church where one can exercise daily and weekly what he has learned from the Word of God. If it is not, it's going to end up in dry rot, just so many outlines, so many books and so many degrees.

I think of the sermon by Paul on Mars Hill. He said they were a very religious people and he came to declare to them who the unknown God was. They had an altar, but left out god, spelled with a small "g", so he said he came to tell them who this altar represented. He put the name to the God—he said He's the Creator God. There's only one God. Idols do not have power of creation. Everyone whom God has created has an infinity with God by creation. No idol can ever cause any personal response, because they are only figments of imagination. Man makes a god in his own sinful image. Paul made it plain, you have to start with the Creator God, and also He's a Governor God. Then he said you have a Father God. These points are the most needed and perhaps most of them are absent in the general preaching and teaching of Christianity today—more than any other points. We are the offspring of God, no offspring of idols.

Everyone that professes to be born again and takes his place as a member of a church is under the rule of the Word of God. We are all vessels. We are supposed to be filled vessels. My father used to drive an old lumber wagon loaded with grain to town. As he was going a little distance from the farm, you could hear nothing, but when he would be coming back, you could hear that lumber wagon coming back empty for a half a mile. Many times empty vessels make more noise than those that are filled with the Spirit. We are instruments in the hand of God.

Chapter 7

Testimony of Mrs. Florence Clearwaters

Pillsbury College Luncheon 1987

When I came in and saw such a lovely arrangement, all the lovely decorations and such a delicious luncheon, I thought they really should have had a real speaker today. Eva Jean said to me on the way in, "I was so surprised to see your name, that you were going to speak to us, because," she said (she knows me well) "I know you don't like to speak," and she could have added "and can't!" But I'm always glad to give a testimony. I've had a long life, perhaps that's why I fit into the Victorian theme here today!

We've been married almost fifty-two years, and it seems like, and many people have expressed it, that we have had pretty much of a

Mrs. Florence Clearwaters.

struggle, but we've had a long and very blessed time and looking back, I guess I wouldn't have changed it.

The greatest highlight in my life, of course, was my salvation. I was twenty-two years old when I was saved. My father was born in Ireland and came over here as a young lad, and my mother was part Irish, and she was Presbyterian and my father was Irish Catholic. Our home could be called somewhat religious, but it certainly wasn't a spiritual home, although it was a good moral home. My father was great on education. He had a very good education. He had a college degree and graduate work, which was not so common back then, and he was so anxious that all of us get a good education and he adequately provided for us.

My struggle began then, after I was saved, and I fell in love with a Baptist preacher, and we were getting married. The family wasn't a bit enthused about that. There wasn't a Baptist anywhere in our family tree, anywhere! My father said he would never be able to support me! That was the first little hurdle I had to make.

My husband had small pastorates. We went to Cedar Rapids, Iowa. That was a very lovely time. The people were wonderful. I knew nothing. Here I was twenty-two years of age. I had a fairly good education. I went to Nazareth College, a private girls' school, for two years. I had nurse's training and took some post-graduate work after that in public health. I thought I had a reasonable education, but when I became a pastor's wife, I realized I needed Bible education. I needed a Bible school. I had no Bible, except what I had dug out myself. My husband helped me, and we had correspondence courses from Moody Bible Institute at the Cedar Rapids Church.

Then we moved to Fourth Church. It seemed my husband has been almost destined to become a leader in controversy and struggles. I look back and see how many struggles we've gone through. I don't think we missed a one anywhere. We no more than got to Cedar Rapids and everyone was in the A.B.C. in those days, back in 1935. We came to Fourth Church, and we didn't realize it, but it was a very strong denominational church. My husband had already been elected to an office in the State and National, and he began to see inside workings and wasn't very happy with what he found. And then we came to such a strong church; we didn't realize it was quite as strong missionary-wise and giving-wise to the Convention. Ultimately he had to pull out and pull the church out, and that caused a split, and over one hundred people went out. But the church had been growing all the time even during all this turmoil. We still had several hundred left. It took about two years to get through it and start to build back.

He was a founder in CBFMS. Those were joyous years through there, because we just loved the fellowship and the missionaries, and it was new. Pretty soon he felt led to pull out, not being able from the inside to change it, at least to try to change the course, but that wasn't possible, so that was another struggle. I think that was the one that was very hard on me, because I had very dear friends, missionary friends, in that group, because we worked very hard and because he had been a founding father of it.

About that time I think the Lord wanted to get our attention off all the negative parts and struggle part. There was nothing my husband could change. You can't change an institution or movement after it gets well started. Someone has said, and my husband has repeated it often, any movement that has departed from its purpose, historically, has never been reversed and gone back to its first position. Here he was, and somehow they always pressured him to be in the forefront. One time we were coming back from something, and I said to my husband, "Wouldn't it be nice if some time you had the role of a hero instead of a villain." And he said, "I don't know if that will ever come." But I was sympathetic with him, because I knew what he was going through, and I knew why.

In the early '50s the Lord brought something into our lives that really took our attention right away from all the controversy in the movements. Our only daughter, Jane, was stricken with polio. It was in the terrible epidemic of 1953. Then immediately nothing mattered but her. We went through months of anguish. She was stricken severely. I bargained with the Lord. I said, "Lord, just don't leave her in a wheelchair." She was an active person. "Let her be up and around. I'll even accept a limp, or anything, but not in a wheelchair." Of course, that was foolish of me to bargain with the Lord, because he had more blessings than I dared to expect. After a great deal of care, etc., she recovered so that you would never know she ever had polio. She's very active. In fact, when she was in Pillsbury, she was on the basketball team.

When we got over that, and that seemed to be a bit of a breaking point, then Northwestern School went through its trials. My husband again was on the board and on the faculty. Dr. Riley failing in health, it was then another crisis in our lives.

The real positive things are when Central Seminary was formed and Pillsbury College. Those were great days, but struggling days. People kept saying to my husband, "You can't do it. You won't have enough money to do it; the people won't be with you." No positive things, until he got going good, and then they were right along with him. But when he was struggling, he was pretty much alone. Then the radio station came along, and they said, "You'll never get a permit, and if you do, you won't be able to find a place to build a tower, and if you do get it up, you'll never be able to afford to operate it." The Lord led in every step.

While we were going through all of this, my husband was meeting with building committees and architects, and we were building five great buildings. Don Nelson talked my husband into three hundred sixty acres of land along the St. Croix, and my husband said, "Don, we have so many things going, we can't do that." But Don isn't one that is easily defeated either, and we went along, and it was paid for in a very short time outside the budget. Then the Christian Day School came along, and that took some doing, and my husband was the budget boy for all of this. As I look back, I don't know how he did it really, because he was so busy all the time. But the Lord was very gracious to us. We had blessings on every side. We had discouragements and struggles, but our blessings far outnumbered our defeats, and we were learning. We were certainly being blessed.

Then in 1980 came another turning point. My husband was always so strong and robust. He would go on planes and trips so sick that he should have been home in bed, but no, he would not cancel appointments.

Fiftieth wedding anniversary, April 1985.

One Sunday morning about 9:30 down at church he broke his wrist. He went to the doctor and got it taken care of and was back in the pulpit at 11:00 and preached a sermon. He never took a pain pill because he said it might not keep his head clear. I thought that was ridiculous, and I told him so. That was one time I didn't agree with him as a nurse.

He had just a slight stroke in 1980, and the Lord was saying, "Now, that's enough." Then in 1981 they discovered that I had cancer of the lung, and that's kinda scary, you know. So I said to the Lord, "Thank you, I've lived a long time, and the Lord's been good to me." But I wanted to stay around and take care of my husband. I said to the Lord, "Well, if that's Your will, I'm ready." The Lord brought me through that; it's been five years now.

The next year my husband fell and fractured his hip in Florida, and received a very poor repair job. We got back and had to have it all done over again.

So those are the years the Lord really spoke to us. We had to realize that our days of hard work were over. But through it all the Lord has been a special blessing.

Lowell Thomas said once, "There were giants on the earth in those days." I feel that I have lived through an era when there were giants on the earth in those days. One of the blessings I have had is that our home has been blessed with such people staying overnight and for dinner as Dr. Ironside, Dr. Gypsy Smith, Homer Rodeheaver, Louie Talbot, Bob Jones, Sr. (Louie Talbot I kept for a week), and many others, Dr. McGinlay, really great warriors of the faith. Plus all the missionaries we've had in our home. And all the students from Pillsbury, they've been a blessing. I always planned for quite a few on Sunday, and I said to Jane to just bring any of the students. I always had a great big table. One time I noticed one young man sitting down at the long table. He wasn't saying a word, and had his head down, and I was getting up and down and serving the guests. Pretty soon I said to Jane, "I don't think I've met this young man." Jane looked at him and said, "Well, I don't know him either." The poor fellow just could have died. One of the other young fellows spoke up and said, "Oh, he's my cousin from St. Paul. He just came over to see me." Those were fun days when we had all the young people coming to our house, as well as all the great people.

Our retirement years are not golden, I'll tell you, but we have wonderful memories.

Dr. Bob Jones, Sr., Dr. R.V. Clearwaters, Dr. John R. Rice.

Dr. Joseph Rammel, Dr. James Mercer, Dr. R.V. Clearwaters.

Dr. Glen Schunk, Dr. R.V. Clearwaters.

Dr. Harriet Bratrud

Chapter 8

Recognition Service on Retirement of Dr. Clearwaters

April 4, 1982

Mr. Bill Campbell presiding: At this time I would like to introduce Kellar Nyquist, who will have a history of Dr. Richard V. Clearwaters here at Fourth Baptist Church, and then two testimonials by past members of Fourth Baptist Church, Dr. C. Wilbur Peters and Mr. Edmund Sansovini. Thank You.

Mr. Kellar Nyquist: January 1940 marked the beginning of the ministry of Dr. Richard V. Clearwaters as pastor of Fourth Baptist Church, a ministry that has endured and prospered through these many years. To appreciate what has been accomplished under his leadership we should go back to the beginning of our church's history and set the stage for his arrival in 1940. We have just finished celebrating our centennial year here at Fourth.

In 1881 this work began as a mission Sunday School in the Jewitt

Chapel at 11th and Lyndale Avenues North. Since that beginning the church has moved twice, first to 18th and Dupont in 1885, then in 1919 to the building which houses Clearwaters Chapel. The Sunday School building north of the chapel was dedicated in 1940 when Dr. and Mrs. Clearwaters came. They moved here from Cedar Rapids, Iowa, where he had pastored the Calvary Baptist Church, having also served in churches in Michigan and Illinois. He became the ninth pastor of this church. His ministry of over forty-two years eclipses by a number of years any of the former pastorates.

Much has changed since he came in 1940. Three of the five buildings in this complex were completed after that. The gymnasium and the school facility to the northwest was erected in 1966. More Sunday School and Day School facilities were completed in 1970, and the new auditorium was dedicated in 1973. In addition to that, we now have a new Seminary library below this auditorium and spacious and up-to-date facilities for the radio station.

But more than the size of our facilities are the programs we use them for. Within these buildings have arisen the many facets of this church's ministry. Sunday School, mission support, calling, youth programs were established before the pastor came and have continued throughout these forty-two years. A 350-acre wilderness camp was purchased on the St. Croix River in Wisconsin. Camping facilities and a large year-round up-to-date lodge were built for use by all the organizations of the church, but primarily for the youth program. WCTS-FM was granted a license to broadcast in 1965 and today is on the air fourteen hours a day, seven days a week.

It has been very evident that Dr. Clearwaters has placed a high value on Christian education through the years. He is the founder of Central Baptist Theological Seminary which operates in these facilities. It began in 1956 and has trained over 300 pastors and other full-time Christian workers who serve in churches and Christian schools throughout the country. Central currently has one of the largest enrollments of any seminary in this area. The pastor started the Bible Institute meeting on Monday nights, which gives lay people an opportunity to systematically study the Bible in a classroom setting. This program serves our people as well as many people from churches in the surrounding area.

Pillsbury Baptist Bible College was established largely through his efforts. He served as its first president, later as chairman of the board, and now serves as president emeritus. Pillsbury trains hundreds of young men and women from all across the country for Christian service. And, of course, largely because of Dr. Clearwaters' foresight, a Christian Day School was started here which provides Christian education in a traditional setting for six hundred pupils, kindergarten through twelfth grade.

It is clear to see that under his leadership Fourth Baptist has experienced substantial growth in facilities and membership and has expanded its ministries in many directions. God has truly blessed this man's work among us.

I Corinthians 4:2, "Moreover it is required in stewards, that a man be found faithful." Dr. Clearwaters has been a faithful servant these forty-three years, to the Lord first, and to the people of Fourth Baptist Church. He is a Bible scholar, a fearless warrior, a zealous soul-winner, a spiritual watchman, a faithful shepherd, a trustworthy counsellor, a beloved father, and an unfailing friend.

Dr. Wilbur Peters: "For other foundation can no man lay than that is laid, which is Jesus Christ." I Corinthians 3:11.

Dr. Clearwaters over the years has used that verse in his ministry to us. When asked to give a testimonial for Dr. Clearwaters, I look back over twenty years of association that I and my family have had with him, and I see many different faces of Dr. Clearwaters.

First of all, I see the face of a preacher of the Word. I'm so thankful that through these many years he has been faithful to the Word. And has preached the whole counsel of the book that has been given to us. I'm thankful that he has been a Biblicist, and he has depended upon the Bible for his teachings and not the teachings of men.

Also, I recognize that as a pastor, he is a great scholar, not only of the Bible, having memorized considerable portions of it, but also a scholar of history and has such a tremendous flair for bringing things of the past into focus for the future regarding our everyday lives. Then, too, he is a scholar of literature. His quotes from the classics have always been a great inspiration and help in bringing the Word to us. Then, too, a scholar of humor. Seldom does a sermon preached here from this pulpit not have humor which brings the truth he is trying to bring into clearer focus to our minds.

I've always appreciated that he has been jealous of his pastorate here. I don't recall one time over these twenty years I have known him in the ministry here that Dr. Clearwaters when present in the service hasn't preached, unless for special revival meetings. In fact, I recall an incident one time when prior to Sunday School he was climbing up on a stool in order to reach some books in the Seminary office, fell off and broke his arm, made a trip to the hospital and had it put in a cast and still preached in the morning service. The doctor said, "Now, you must keep your arm in the air." And so we had a message that morning with a one-armed Moses giving us the Word from God, holding that arm up through the entire sermon. I appreciated that faithfulness of Dr. Clearwaters in his ministry as a pastor.

Next, I saw the face of an educator. Not only was he a Seminary professor in his earlier years, but he founded Central Seminary, and later Pillsbury College, and then the Christian Day School, and he has been a writer of books. The face of the educator certainly came through clearly as I thought back over my association with him.

Then, I saw the face of an administrator. Not only does he administer faithfully with his staff and has had tremendous cooperation over the years from them, but he has a remarkable understanding of finances, which I appreciate in the heart of a pastor. He also has a good understanding of the business world—not only the finances of the church, but he understands business and its workings. Also he has had an excellent relationship with the Northside Community and was involved in community affairs. He worked over the years in making West Broadway a better business place and a better place for each of its citizens.

Obviously, you cannot look at Dr. Clearwaters and not see the face of a soul-winner. He always supported the Sunday School tremendously. I don't recall that I ever came out for a calling meeting on a Tuesday night that Dr. and Mrs. Clearwaters were not there making calls with us. His personal soul-winning over the years we all know about, the contacts he has made and the people he has won to the Lord in his personal witnessing.

Again, I see the face of a politician. Many people think that a politician is negative, but Dr. Clearwaters has never played politics;

rather, Dr. Clearwaters engaged in politics. Politics is a very important part of a church organization, as well as it is in the business world, that is, preparing the people for the things that are to come. Politicians are people that we entrust to carry out the wishes of the people. Dr. Clearwaters had an uncanny ability to do that over the years. I remember his talking for two or three years prior to the founding of our Christian Day School. It was a matter of training and educating each of us to accept the fact that we needed to sacrifice for the benefit of our families and the education of our children to have a Christian Day School. And, of course, before I was part of Fourth Baptist Church, Dr. Clearwaters led this church out of the American Baptist Association, out of the CBA and was involved in many other things. He has an uncanny understanding of the trend of national affairs.

There are many other faces, but let me close with the fact that as I look at Dr. Clearwaters I see the face of a personal friend. When I first knew Dr. Clearwaters and became a member of Fourth Baptist Church, I was a fledgling business man and we shared many things over the years, and Dr. Clearwaters was a great help and inspiration to me in my early years. And then as the years went by, as Doc would so often say, we poured coffee frequently and we poured our hearts out to each other—concerns about the church, concerns about the Lord's business, as well as my own personal business which we had dedicated to the Lord. And we certainly have appreciated the opportunity, my wife and I and family, of having sat under the ministry of Dr. Clearwaters over these years.

And we know that officially he is retiring as pastor of Fourth Baptist Church, but we all recognize that he's not retiring from the Lord's work, and we expect that we are going to hear many good things about Dr. Clearwaters in the years to come. We certainly appreciate the opportunity of our fellowship with him and sitting under his ministry these many years.

Mr. Edmund Sansovini: Wilbur touched on personal witnessing and concern for souls. I'm here as a personal testimony to Dr. Clearwaters. I remember the first call he ever made on our house back in 1948. I was a young businessman at the time, interested in material things. He called on us and opened the Word of God and kept calling; he was very very persistent. My wife and I eventually came to a saving knowledge of Jesus

Dr. R.V. Clearwaters with Ed Sansovini.

Christ through his personal witness and his personal love for our souls.

We had the privilege of serving seventeen years in this church from the day we were saved. I appreciated the fact that Dr. Clearwaters and Roger Peterson recognized a young man and gave him an opportunity, and we became active in the Sunday School, particularly in the area of promotion, and it was a real joy to work in that area for several years before the Lord led us elsewhere.

I was sitting down the other day before coming up here, and I penned some words I would like to share with you as a testimony to this church and particularly to Dr. Clearwaters:

> I'm here this afternoon to honor a man who has honored God and His Word. I am here to honor the man who coined the word "Biblicist" and gave it true meaning and content. I am here to honor a man who has been loyal to the Bible, and because he has been

loyal to the Bible, I have been loyal to him. I am here to honor a man who is a good minister of Jesus Christ, who illustrates precepts by example and illuminates truths with his life. I am here to honor a man who is a great defender of the faith, one who rightly divides the Word of God. I am here to honor a man who is a true shepherd of the flock. I am here to honor the man who is one of the reasons I am able to stand in this pulpit today and testify to the saving grace of Jesus Christ. Through his personal witness my family circle is complete in Christ.

Permit me to take you through a few memorable moments in our relationship. They are a testimony to this church and to the ministry of this great man:

In 1948 Dr. Clearwaters came into our lives. I was not a Christian at the time. I was a young man searching, but through his personal witness we became Christians.

December 3, 1949, my wife Jean, who unfortunately couldn't be here today, was saved in evangelistic meetings conducted by Dr. John R. Rice. A day later, December 4, 1949, I accepted Jesus Christ and walked the aisle of the old auditorium. II Corinthians 5:17 became a reality in my life and my lifetime verse. Dr. Clearwaters' persistence and prayers were answered.

December 24, 1949, Christmas Eve, my wife and I were baptized by Dr. Clearwaters. We became active members of this church. Our daughters, Pat and Betty, were dedicated to the Lord here in this church.

1952, I started to teach my first Sunday School class.

1956, our daughter Kathy was born and dedicated to the Lord.

1958, and this was a real highlight as a father, our son, Richard was born. And we didn't have to decide who we were going to name him after. We named him after the one who meant so much to us, Dr. Clearwaters. He was dedicated to the Lord later that year.

1959, the beginning of many promotional efforts for the church and Sunday School in which I was privileged to be a part.

1960, our daughter Kathy went home to be with the Lord. Dr. Clearwaters trained us well. He taught us to accept this as the will of God and claim Romans 8:28.

1962, our Sunday morning service was televised for the first time.

1964, we set a new Sunday School record of 823.

1965, we set a new Sunday School record of 900. The Lord led us to St. Louis. However, we still assisted Fourth in their Sunday School efforts. It was a great privilege for us, even though we were miles away, to come up two or three times a year to assist this great church.

1966, we set a new Sunday School record of 1253.

1967, we set a new Sunday School record of 1440. There were 189 decisions, including 122 for salvation.

1967 through 1982, Dr. Clearwaters and I remained very close friends. We always looked forward to the letters and the phone calls and the February vacation periods which always allowed us to fellowship together.

The Lord has allowed us to have thirty-four wonderful years of friendship, loyalty and labor together. Thank you, Dr. Clearwaters, for allowing me to be your friend and to share these few moments in your honor.

Rev. Don Nelson, who as you know was youth pastor of this church for many years, is in the balcony televising this program, and he has asked me to make a presentation on behalf of his church and mission board. This placque, Dr. Clearwaters, is presented to you and Mrs. Clearwaters, and it reads:

> "Presented to Dr. and Mrs. Clearwaters, pastor and first lady of the Fourth Baptist Church, Minneapolis, Minnesota, in recognition and honor of forty-two years of exemplary service, founder and president of Pillsbury Baptist Bible College, founder and president of Central Baptist Theological Seminary, presented by Bethany Baptist Church, Fort Lauderdale, Florida, and the Independent Baptist Caribbean Mission and Institute, Donald E. Nelson." There are three Scripture verses: Psalm 138:2; I Timothy 3:16; and Isaiah 8:20. It is dated April 4, 1982.

Mr. Bill Campbell: Thank you gentlemen. At this time representing Fourth Baptist Church, remarks by Rev. Roger Peterson, Minister of Christian Education; Mr. Bill Reed, Chairman of the Deacon Board; Mr. Donald Ogilvie, Chairman of the Trustee Board; and Mr. Jeff

Benson, Registrar of Central Seminary.

Rev. Roger Peterson: Thank you, Bill Campbell. I want to turn to Psalm 81:10. I think it fits Dr. Clearwaters well. "I am the Lord thy God which brought thee out of the land of Egypt. Open thy mouth wide, and I will fill it."

I think of Dr. Clearwaters coming out of Egypt, the Northern Baptist Convention, long before I came here. I thank God for that. I read history about it, and I appreciate what he has delivered us from. And Mrs. Clearwaters standing with him in all the trials that went with that. Praise God for our school and for our church that was able to come out of that.

God said, "If you come out, I will fill your mouth." And He did. "Open your mouth wide, and I will fill it." God has filled his mouth with many good things here at Fourth Baptist Church. He has allowed him to establish many things about which you have heard already. As a result, Dr. Clearwaters, you have been a great blessing to my own life and to my family's life.

We came here because you opened up Central Seminary. We had no intention of joining Fourth Baptist Church. When Central Seminary opened, I was only going to come for one year. But God used this to change my life. My wife and I had just gotten married that summer, so when we came here we were just a brand new family. God used Central Seminary first of all, to deliver me from interdenominationalism and from New Evangelicalism. I was getting trapped in that, and I praise God that Central Seminary delivered me from that. Not only that, but Central Seminary gave me the tools to prepare me for the ministry. And Central Seminary was a blessing because after I graduated, I was able to serve in the school. So Central Seminary has meant a lot to me, having come here in the very first year that it opened.

Then, that year I also joined Fourth Baptist Church, along with my wife, in December 1956. As a result we heard you preach and were able to fellowship with your people. You taught us to be separatists, and you taught us to give sacrificially, and you taught us how to take care of our families. We didn't have much of a family yet, just my wife and I, but we were to have three sons.

You established Camp Clear-Waters. There we were able to minister, and many, many from our church went out there and were greatly

Dr. and Mrs. R.V. Clearwaters, 1976.

blessed. Finally, my sons were old enough to go out, and at fifteen years of age, my oldest son accepted Christ as Saviour there at camp. Many others accepted Christ as Saviour at camp. You've blessed many, many lives. You opened your mouth wide and blessed my life and my family, praise God for that.

You saw fit to establish a Christian Day School, which has blessed not only my family, but many others. When you opened the school, my oldest son, Philip, started the first year; he had gone one year to the public school. Soon my second son started, and they both graduated from the Christian Day School. My last son, Mark, is about ready to graduate this year, the Lord willing. Praise God. I had no idea it would be this great a blessing when you started that school.

Not only that, but you had the foresight to establish WCTS. By faith you applied for an application and by faith you established this radio station as a companion in our home and in our car. This has been a blessing to our whole family. A great life has come into our home as a result of WCTS. And this is just one family of many multitudes who have been so blessed.

Not only that, but you established Pillsbury Baptist Bible College. Long before I had children, you established it, and I supported it the first year. My brother went to that school. I am sorry he didn't stay, because he would have been under the good ministry of Dr. Parker. Then the Lord sent us children. We waited. The Lord sent them through Christian Day School. We waited. Finally, we got our first son in and now he is in his fourth year at Pillsbury. Our second son is in his second year, and next year we will have our third son at Pillsbury Baptist Bible College. I praise God for that school.

You said you did not want to shout at the darkness. Many fundamentalists have. They preach from the pulpit but they do nothing more than preach. You didn't shout at the darkness. God bless you for following through, lighting lamps that would dispel the darkness. You've opened your mouth wide and God filled it. You set a light out in this area that has blessed our family. It's a blessing that my wife and I want to share with you along with many others of our church. We thank you for lighting these lamps. We ask God to bless you, and we know He is going to bless you and Mrs. Clearwaters and your daughter. And you shall shine as the brightness of the firmament and as the stars forever and ever. Thank you for bringing light into our family.

Mr. Bill Reed: On this 4th day of April, 1982, we the Deacon Board of Fourth Baptist Church have voted unanimously to commend Dr. and Mrs. Richard V. Clearwaters for almost forty-three years of ministry here. It can be said of them with Paul the Apostle, "I have fought a good fight, I have finished my course, I have kept the faith: Henceforth there is laid up for me a crown of righteousness." They are known for their stand on the Bible as Biblicists, and it is with this fundamental characteristic, we as a church have been led to know and to do the work of the Lord. Our church is known across the nation and around the world. Many churches have asked when they were uncertain, "How would Fourth Baptist do that?" or, "What would Dr. Clearwaters do in that situation?" This mark of leadership is foremost in our hearts and minds. We have grown to love Dr. and Mrs. Clearwaters. Therefore, we honor them for the faithful stand and leadership in the Word of God in this local church.

Mr. Donald Ogilvie: Dr. Clearwaters has been my pastor for twenty-one years. In just that amount of time I've seen the building increase in size about seventy-five percent, parking lots added, Christian Day School, WCTS went on the air, a fleet of buses purchased, and a youth camp developed with many facilities. Pastor McLachlan has said that he can think of nowhere that a pastor could inherit a better plant than we have right here, requiring only maintenance for many years. In I Corinthians 4:2 we read, "Moreover it is required in stewards that a man be found faithful." Dr. and Mrs. Clearwaters for forty-two years have been faithful as spiritual and financial leaders in this church. Dr. Clearwaters has attended all the trustee meetings, worked many hours fighting many battles to preserve the work going on right here. Mrs. Clearwaters has taught Sunday School and led many ladies' groups in the Seminary and in the church. On behalf of the trustees and the members of Fourth Baptist Church, I would like to thank Dr. and Mrs. Clearwaters for their many years of faithful leadership. It's been a great honor for me and a pleasure for me to serve with you, Dr. Clearwaters. Thank you.

Mr. Jeff Benson: In thinking of this service, my mind went to Ecclesiastes 2:18, 19, where Solomon expresses from a wholly natural viewpoint the anxieties a man faces as he must deliver his life's work to a successor. Solomon says this, "Yea, I hated all my labor which I had taken under the sun: because I should leave it unto the man that shall be after me. And who knoweth whether he shall be a wise man or a fool? yet, shall he have rule over all my labor wherein I have labored, and wherein I have showed myself wise under the sun. This is also vanity."

We praise God that this ministry built here for forty-two years is not simply one man's work under the sun, but this ministry has been wrought in the power of the Spirit of God and shrouded in the providence of God. Thus the future of this ministry need not be faced anxiously, but in confident trust in God. It's a marvelous credit as I look at Doc's ministry here that he can now pass his ministry on to a man who stands as a product of two schools which he has founded, Pillsbury College and Central Baptist Seminary. Thus, the Biblical distinctives that have characterized the ministry of Dr. Clearwaters will continue to be upheld.

We at Central Seminary wish to express our love, our gratitude and our deep appreciation to Dr. Clearwaters for his twenty-six years of leadership in the Seminary and for the Biblical distinctives which he has stamped upon all aspects of his ministry. These distinctives as I see them are fourfold: number 1, the primacy of the local church; number 2, personal and ecclesiastical separation; number 3, faithful commitment to the whole counsel of the Word of God, which has made him first a Biblicist and second a fundamentalist and a Baptist. But the greatest thing I have learned from Dr. Clearwaters and am impressed with as I've worked with him for the past few years in the Seminary, is simply his love for the ministry and his love for souls. Often I've seen him in tears and in great concern for us and for this church and for the people here. We appreciate this small part in honoring him, and we convey our sincere appreciation and deep thanks to Dr. Clearwaters for his service to us and dedication to God's Word.

(This service concluded with Mr. Charles Pratt presenting to Dr. and Mrs. Clearwaters a grandfather clock and a cash gift.)

Mr. Charles Pratt: We hope that you both have many years ahead, and we give you our thanks once again and our Christian love, and may God bless both of you. We would like to have you say a few words.

Mrs. Clearwaters: I will just say "thank you".

Response by Dr. Clearwaters

I have been many times during the service feeling like crying and laughing. I appreciate the great attendance I see here, which was a surprise to me. I was telling someone yesterday and again today when I read the many congratulations and expressions of appreciation that came to me both from friend and foe, I said it made me feel like reconsidering and staying! But I'm not going to do that.

I appreciate this great attendance. I appreciate the program and those who have had a part in it. They were most generous. I think I should let you in on one or two little secrets. One, few people realize that I was received and taken into Bible conference work at a relatively young age. I really was honored to stand with some of the great giants of the past. For example, someone referred here to something that made me think I heard one time a message from the only person I ever heard speak on a spirit of discernment. A whole message by Dr. Bob Jones, Sr. and I was so impressed that I from that moment on prayed more often, "God, Oh, God, make me to do better than I know." As I summed up his message, that was what he was trying to get across to us. And his argument was that if you can't do better than you know, the world gets help from downstairs, and we have to get help from upstairs. If we get that prayer answered, we will have that spirit of discernment.

Then again, I want to share something else with you—a second principle. I admired A.J. Gordon. He was a generation ago, founder of the Gordon School of Theology and Missions. When I had the first opportunity in Boston, I wanted to go to the Clarendon Street Church and visit where he ministered and where he gave birth to that school. I did. I came into that old auditorium still in the trappings of the gay 90s, the old faded pew cushions. I understood that a student was holding forth in this church with possibly forty people. What really moved me was, forward as you faced the pulpit, was a bronze bust of A.J. Gordon, in the midst of the trappings of the gay 90s. The school had moved on and didn't have enough interest in the founder to move the likeness of the founder still standing. It took me back to a Bible Conference in New York where I was preaching. I was preaching among household names—you would know most of them. Few of them would know me. But one of them, who was the elect president of the Gordon School of Theology and Missions, roomed with me in the hotel, that is, next door, not in the same room. But he chose me out. He wanted to have lunch with me and he wanted to advise me. He was just beginning his work as president of the Gordon School of Theology and Missions. He said, "You're a younger man." He went on to compliment me. He thought I had this, that and the other—a brilliant mind and great insight, etc., but he said, "I want to warn you. You are a militant, and militancy will not be received in our day." I said, "Do you think Paul apologized when he said, I bear in my body the marks of the Lord Jesus?" And we spent a very interesting two hours at lunch. Neither one of us got his point across. I stood on the Word of God, and he stood on the reasoning of men—you've got to soft-pedal, you've got to be all things to all men, you've got to find a middle ground, you can't be dogmatic. May I tell you, this is why you've got the Gordon-Conwell School today that would not be recognized by the man represented by that bust. They didn't think enough of him to take the likeness of the founder with them.

This is kind of a parable. These are the things that go through a man's mind. And it's possible to happen anywhere. I said I have perfect peace about the one who succeeds me, and I have great confidence. God has given me great peace. I have no emotional proxism about my resignation. I might say now that if I have a spirit of discernment, I was set out on this by another, and if I have, for example, been persistent in militancy, that is the one principle that has caused all of this to take place. Militancy on the basis of the Word of God. And it is really to me very satisfying that men I have worked with for years, like Dr. Parker and Dr. Rammel, and many others that could be named, that I have been blamed for their doings and they have been blamed for mine, because we both think after the thoughts of God in this Book. Two things equal to the same thing are equal to each other. Though that is a mathematical principle, it's an ideological principle as well, and when this is the final source of our authority, we naturally are going to have the same aims and ambitions and principles. But the poor undiscerning world reasoning after men does not understand this.

I had other things I was going to say, but I may have another opportunity to speak later sometime on this, but I wanted to leave those two things with you.

Dr. and Mrs. R.V. Clearwaters, 1982.

Again, I express my great appreciation to the followship of Fourth Baptist Church. Many of you were not here this morning, but at your own churches, but I used as a text this morning, and I close with it. It fits the ministry I had here. Paul was speaking. "And ye became followers of us, and of the Lord, having received the word in much affliction, with joy of the Holy Ghost." I Thess. 1:6. Ye have become followers of us. Many times it is difficult for people to follow a militant leader, and they have to become followers. It is not a gift; it's progressive. And so it is first of all then, an act of faith for the followers to follow the militant leader, but it's also following the Lord. In others words, the Lord is the object of their faith when they are following. Then, having received the word in much affliction, speaks of the endurance of faith. The act of faith, the object of faith, the endurance of faith, the joy of faith. There is no joy like it, and the Holy Ghost is the power of faith. I promised them this morning that sometime I would share a good textual sermon on that. I used it this morning as a topical sermon, which I warn my students to use very seldom.

I thank the church for these gifts. We are grateful for these things that will be a great help in remembering and calling to remembrance many of you, and this from the alumni. Words fail me on this occasion to express my deep appreciation, and I would say this, as I said before, we continue to live here. This is our home. This people are still in our hearts. And as I said in my resignation, if at any time I become a hindrance, we would remove ourselves. If we can give any help, we stand ready.

Again to all of you I say thank you. And by the way, about this clock, it spoils a lot of arguments I've made. My wife's been talking about a clock for a long time and I've said, "You just don't have room for it." I suppose that clock has broken down all my arguments. All my logic has failed!

The Lord has been so very gracious in so many ways. We cannot deny His grace and His love.

Don Nelson is here doing audio-visual. He asked me if I would write in his Bible. These words had been an inspiration:

> I'm walking on the upward way
> For that still holds the sun.
> I'm climbing the night pastures
> Where the starry river runs.
> And if you seek to find me
> In the old and dark abode,
> You'll find it written on the door
> "I'm on the upward road."

Remarks of Dr. Monroe Parker
Director of Baptist World Mission
April 4, 1982

I feel something like the man who said he cut the tail off the lion with his pocket knife. Somebody said that was a very courageous thing to do, but why didn't you cut off his head?" "Well," he said, "somebody else had already done that."

I did not prepare a message like Dr. Rammel because I was the second speaker, in fact, the last of a number of speakers, and I thought I would just pick up the chips, because they will say so many wonderful things about Dr. Clearwaters and Mrs. Clearwaters, because there are so many wonderful things to say about them.

I first knew Dr. Clearwaters back in 1943; whether he remembers, I do. I held meetings in St. Paul with Dr. Murk. I came over to Northwestern Schools and met Dr. Clearwaters there. He had students down in Bob Jones University in my preachers' class from Fourth Baptist, and then he came down there and spoke at the college and also in the preachers' class and became a real man whom I admired greatly. Of course, I heard from the students who were from his church so many wonderful things about him. I got better acquainted when I came up to preach for the Minnesota Baptist Convention in 1956 and later held meetings at Fourth Baptist Church.

I have been with Dr. Clearwaters on so many occasions and always when you ask him how he feels, he says, "Just fine!" I've never heard one complaint out of him about his feelings in all the association I've had with him. He's been a real inspiration to me, and all the things that have been said about him I can vouch that they're true.

Of course, you can't move without producing friction, and I've noticed that the faster you move, the more friction you produce. Dr. Clearwaters has been blamed for many things he had nothing to do with. I know that to be true. I served four years as President of the Minnesota Baptist Convention. Not once did Dr. Clearwaters suggest to me what I ought to do in all that time, and he was on the Executive Committee, too. He'd always attend, but not one time did he ever make a suggestion, and yet he was blamed for many things I did. And I served almost eight years (seven years and eight months) as President of Pillsbury College, and he got the blame for many things I did down there that he had nothing to do with.

When I was elected, he wrote me a letter and he said, "You can put this in your file." It was a letter of resignation from the Board. "If I ever get in your way, you can just tell me that you have accepted my resignation." Well, I didn't want to accept that resignation; in fact, I thanked God everyday he was Chairman of the Board.

But he who ascends to mountain tops must find the loftiest peaks, most wrapped in clouds and snow; he who surpasses or subdues mankind must look down on the hatred of those below.

Of course, if you move as fast as Dr. Clearwaters has moved and do as much has he has done, you cause a great deal of friction, and there'll be some people who don't appreciate it, but this testimony today is just a small expression of the thousands of people over the country who praise God for the ministry of Dr. Clearwaters and for the blessing he has been in their lives. I meet them all over the United States. Nearly everywhere I go, and I'm in full-time evangelism. I go from the north to the south and from the east to the west and almost everywhere I go I run into somebody that tells me he is from Fourth Baptist Church, or used to be there, and many, many of them were saved in Fourth Baptist Church.

I thank God for Mrs. Clearwaters and her faithfulness and the example she has been to many young ladies in the Seminary and down at Pillsbury College and many people throughout the Minnesota Baptist Convention. I count it a great honor to be here today in this effort to honor Dr. and Mrs. Clearwaters, and I'm glad to see their daughter, Jane, who is an alumna of Pillsbury and has a wonderful record there.

Dr. Clearwaters was not only Chairman of the Board, but also the first President of Pillsbury Baptist Bible College, which he retrieved from modernism, and that is unique. It's the only institution I know of that was retrieved from modernism. When it was an academy, and I've seen a pamphlet of some of the teachings that were going on down there, they were even teaching against the virgin birth. And Dr. Clearwaters retrieved that institution. He had to go to court to do it, but he did and founded Pillsbury Baptist Bible College. We thank God for that.

One has said that every institution is the length and shadow of its founder. These great institutions will go on until Jesus comes, and they are truly the shadow of Dr. Clearwaters. I was just thinking about the many things he has done, like founding the camp named Camp Clear-Waters (he did not name it), and the broadcasting station, and all these institutions, and they will continue.

Now this would be a sad day if it were the end of Dr. Clearwaters' ministry, but it's not. He is still greatly involved in the Seminary and will remain there. There is a sense in which it is sad because he is retiring from the pastorate of this great church, which he has made one of the greatest churches in America. Sad for that reason, yet a glad day because of the fine man God has sent to succeed him, one whom he himself highly recommends and whom the church has unanimously called. What a wonderful thing and how wise he is in getting this man here while he is still living where he can be a help to him as he continues here in the church. I'm sure, knowing Dr. Clearwaters as I do having been a colleague of his, Dr. Clearwaters will not be a burden, but a great help to the new pastor.

Jesus said, "He that honoreth me, him will my Father honor." That's why Dr. Clearwaters is being honored today. He honors the Lord Jesus Christ and has in all his preaching and in everything I've known him to do through these years I have been connected with him and known him as a colleague. Thank you.

Chapter 9

Response by Dr. Clearwaters

on Being Named Pastor Emeritus of Fourth Baptist Church 1982

Pactor McLachlan: Tonight is a special opportunity for us to honor in a special way one of God's servants here at Fourth Baptist Church, Dr. Richard V. Clearwaters, pastor of this church for some forty-two years. I believe he became the pastor in 1940, and I often remark that I was born in 1941. All the days of my life he has been the pastor of this church. It certainly is a great privilege, and in a sense, an awesome responsibility to be his successor here in this ministry. Tonight we are conferring upon him the honorary title of "Pastor Emeritus" of Fourth Baptist Church, and we are delighted to be able to do that.

Dr. Clearwaters: Thank you, Pastor McLachlan. Some months ago

Pastor McLachlan came into my office and said he had been thinking of this, and he said he was sure in talking with leaders that it would be the will of the church. And he said at some appropriate time with my consent he would like to have this done. Well, we talked and prayed and as he left, I said, "Now, I'll say nothing about this and," I said, "if you change your mind, I'll not hold you to the promise. All I'm interested in is what may help you as the pastor, help Fourth Baptist Church, and bring glory to God."

Now you want to know how all this happened. I happened to be in the midst of this happening. I happened to be in the right place at the right time when the Lord wanted to do something at 21st and Fremont. He happened to give me a cooperative spirit, and He also gave a cooperative spirit to hundreds of you to go along with His plan. That's how it happened.

Tonight just before coming down here I had a phone call from Western Union. This lady said she had a telegram from Paul Fosmark up in New Brunswick. I said, "Will you read it to me." And she said, "Well, he's congratulating you on being Pastor Emer-i-tus!" My goodness, I said to myself, that sounds like either an infection or maybe inflammation at least! I thanked her and told her to mail it out to me.

I want to thank all of you for coming and each one who has had such a wonderful part in this program and for your adulation and praise for me, which I feel in many ways most unworthy of. Dr. Rammel, I have here my token of "President Emeritus" of Pillsbury College.

I want to have just a little word. You know we believe in expository preaching in Central Seminary, and I want to do a little exposition on that word "emeritus". Once when I was just beginning grade school, my father was near his forge, and he was doing some shimming up of the steel tires on the big lumber wagon. My older brother was helping him. My father referred to the fifth wheel on the wagon. I was full of questions, and finally he had me get under the front end of the wagon and showed me what the fifth wheel was. I said, "This wheel doesn't touch the ground." No. "It doesn't bear any weight." No. "It doesn't even turn around." No. "Well," he said, "It's really not a wheel. We just call it that." So, Pastor Emeritus, we call it a pastor but it's really not a pastor. We have to be honest. I believe, as all of you know, there is one pastor of a New Testament church, and he can pull rank on any member or on any other staff member in that church. I've honored that principle all my life.

I'm most grateful for this occasion, and I'm sure if Mrs. Clearwaters would come here, and I urged her to come and share these remarks, but as you know she is a little backward about speaking in public. But you put a refregerator or a stove in front of her and she's very eloquent! She doesn't always agree with what you say, either. She has her own ideas, and I would have been delighted for her to share some of them. But I want to say that a large measure of my success I've had should rest on her name, too. She's been a very faithful companion through the years, and you heard by the announcement tonight, it'll be about a half century next year, and she has been immeasurable in her service with me. Sometimes a pastor's wife can make great contribution by just keeping still. In fact, I've known a lot of pastors who would have gotten along better if he had had that kind of wife. But, thank God, she has known when to speak and when to be silent. I think of her as the first lady in the church if I'm the first man; we stand together.

Again, I want to thank all of you, the pastor especially, for doing this, and I pledge you what I did when I resigned and he became pastor of the church. I said, "Now, I want your judgment and consent. We have no place to go if we left this church, and," I said, "ex-pastors don't have a very good reputation." I have to face that. I said, "With your consent, we will stay and I'd teach my Sunday School class." He said, "By all means you should. We will be glad to have you." So that has occurred. Then I added this, "If I ever become a problem to you or cause you any trouble, I want you to tell me first, because I can fix it in a hurry."

With those words, I thank God for this opportunity to respond and also for this wonderful placque. Sometime when you get a chance and can come by the office, come in and I'll show you where I display it. Thank you very much, and I'm grateful to those who have had a part. (Standing ovation.)

Chapter 10

Seminary Recognition Service for Dr. Clearwaters, April 6, 1987

President Emeritus, Central Baptist Theological Seminary

Opening remarks, Mr. Charles Pratt: Dr. Richard V. Clearwaters founded Central Baptist Theological Seminary of Minneapolis in 1956. The Seminary began with a full three-year schedule on September 11, and thirty-one students from ten states, studying under a faculty of seven. God's hand was evidenced on the school from the beginning.

As Central grew and developed, its purpose remained steadfast: to prepare at the graduate level men and women whom God has called to His service for a Biblicist witness and work at home and abroad. It was proposed to train these dedicated servants in the faith once for all delivered to the saints, in order that they may emulate the Saviour, who grew in wisdom and stature and in favor with God and man.

By Central's thirtieth anniversary in 1986 nearly five hundred graduates were serving the Lord in the harvest field of the world. Tonight we have friends here of Dr. Clearwaters who will be bringing their testimony to Doc's influence for God in their lives.

I would like to introduce them at this time. They will be presenting their testimonies in this order: first, we will hear from Dr. Fred Moritz. He is no stranger to us. Dr. Moritz is a graduate of Central Seminary, and he is Executive Director of Baptist World Mission. Following Dr. Moritz, we will hear from Dr. Donald E. Nelson, Pastor of Bethany Baptist Church, Fort Lauderdale, Florida, and as you know, a former member of the pastoral staff here at Fourth Baptist. Following Dr. Nelson, we will hear from Dr. Joseph Rammel, President of Pillsbury Baptist Bible College, and certainly a friend of Central Seminary and Fourth Baptist Church. Then we will hear from Rev. Bruce Henry, who is president of the Alumni Association, also a graduate of Central and Pastor of the Ambassador Baptist Church of Shoreview.

Dr. Fred Moritz: It is said that a school is the length and shadow of a man. It was by the grace of God and a great privilege as I spent my days in college and seminary to have the shadow of two men of God fall over my life. I got to Pillsbury College, and there was Dr. Monroe Parker, and his influence on my life has been profound. And then I came to Central Seminary, and I would say that Dr. Clearwaters' influence was no less profound in those days, as a preacher, as a pastor, as a Christian leader, as a counsellor, and as a teacher. One year I was pastoring in Rochester and coming up here to go to Seminary. I ended up taking a lot of Practical Theology, having Dr. Clearwaters for twelve hours in one year.

There are some pithy sayings that Doc had which I have put together in my memory. I remember one time he was telling a story about one of the battles in the Iowa Baptist Convention when he pastored in Cedar Rapids before he came to Minneapolis. And there was a struggle in the modernist-fundamentalist controversy, and I think, Doc, you told us you were chairing the meeting, if I remember correctly. A certain maneuver was made by a modernist, and the parliamentarian chairing the meeting, Dr. Clearwaters, made a ruling. The line that came out (and it was interesting that I heard this line twice in the last twenty-four hours; two different seminary graduates and I were talking and recalled this line), "The fellow didn't know his head was cut off until he tried to spit." That has stuck with several of us over the years.

I remember another one. We had a fellow come to chapel one day. I could tell you his name and I could tell you the church he was preaching in, but I will not embarrass the guilty. He came to Seminary to preach in chapel. It was a wonderous thing! He preached from the 53rd chapter of the book of Isaiah, and in that great passage which is a prophecy of the finished work of the Lord Jesus, this fellow got the entire Pentateuch in the 53rd chapter of Isaiah. Someone after chapel, and we always had that great ritual that still persists—coffee break—someone slipped up to Doc in the hallway and said, "Doc, where in the world did he get that?" And Dr. Clearwaters made an astute observation. He said, "He sucked it out of his thumb."

Then, I can remember a preaching class. He was talking about organization. It must have been after Christmas and he had carried out the Christmas tree and chopped it up for the garbage man. He said, "You know, fellows, there's one difference between a tree and a brush pile—organization. I can't tell you how many times I've heard sermons preached out of the brush pile." That was a pointed lesson.

I think of another one. He was talking about church leadership. And he said, "It's much like riding a horse. When you go to a new church, never use the spurs until you know you are firmly in the saddle." Wise advice.

In talking about dealing with people, I can remember how he would say, reminding him of his farm days when they would drive mules, and the mule got lazy; they would always carry a certain amount of chain to just hit the mule on the back of the feet with. He said, "You know, you can drive mules, but," he said, "sheep have to be led. Sheep resist being driven." Sage advice.

He also used to tell us, "Your people will know if you love them. If they ever get the idea that you don't love them, you're done." How wise! We have found that advice true over the years in the pastorate.

Some years ago I was pastoring in Indianapolis. I'd been there a couple of years. The Chairman of the Deacons took me out to lunch one day and informed me that my ministry was done and it was time for me to resign. He was four and a half years early! I had asked Doc's advice over several months about this. And by the time the man left the church, he was not chairman of the deacons, he was not a deacon, he was sitting on the back row. I was talking with Doc on the phone one day about it, and we had come to a place where things had kind of settled down. And I said, "Doc, it looks like things are better." And he said, "I hope so, but remember something. Diotrephes seldom repents." You know that man is in a church in a state far removed from Indiana doing the same thing today to the pastor that he tried to do to me. Diotrephes seldom repents.

It seems like these little one-liners just stuck!

I remember one day he came to chapel, and after chapel was over, he stood up, and this is the one that really sticks in my mind. He said, "I went to a nursing home yesterday to make some visits. I saw five professions of faith." He had led five folks to Christ in the nursing home the day before. He said, "You know, fellows, nothing, nothing will keep your ministry fresh like weekly contact with the lost." We knew he was a soul-winner. He would say, "The ground is level at the foot of the cross."

I suppose I will remember these little sayings over many years. But the one that sticks in my mind more than any other, and the one I want to close with. There is nothing light about it. Many times he would quote Isaiah 42:8, and the phrase that kept coming up was a natural part of his character. He would say, "We must keep an eye single to God's glory." Many of you are nodding your heads. We have heard that statement hundreds of times. I'm glad I had the privilege of studying under a man who had that kind of concern, which he built into us by his example as well as by his word, that desire to live and to serve to bring glory to God. I'm grateful for the influence he had on my life.

God bless you. Thank you, Doc.

Dr. Donald E. Nelson: Thank you, Dr. Moritz. Just a few weeks ago Dr. Moritz and I were in Haiti, and except for the grace of God and praying friends, we might not be here tonight. We came to one road block, and we didn't know this at the moment, but some fifty-two people were killed in that area during the week we were there. Pray much for the missionaries under Baptist World Mission in Haiti.

I'd like to thank Brother Charles Pratt for according me this privilege to stand here. It's nearly a quarter of a century since I stood here with Dr. Clearwaters as his youth pastor. And these remarks I want to make in reference to his influence upon my life are both individual and they are representative.

I have a verse of Scripture. "Thou therefore, my son, be strong in the grace that is in Christ Jesus. And the things that thou hast heard of me among many witnesses. . . " What are some of the things that Dr. Clearwaters has taught me?

First, he took me from interdenominationalism and I became a Biblicist and a Baptist by conviction. Dr. Clearwaters, I'll always remember that cold wintry day when at the airport you met me and you welcomed me back to this country after five years as a missionary in the Far East. I had written to Dr. Clearwaters, and I said, "Dr. Clearwaters, I'm through with interdenominationalism. I want to be a Baptist, but one that is personified by your position." He reconvened an Ordination

Council, and the most precious document I have is one signed by you, Dr. Clearwaters, and others on the Ordination Council when you and Fourth Baptist Church ordained me as a convicted Biblicist and a Baptist, and I trust that I will never disappoint anybody in that position.

There are two other things Dr. Clearwaters taught me and I have never forgotten them. One of them was the fivefold definition of a pastor. Numbers of times you said, “Most people called to full-time service can preach, and they should be able to teach, but that’s only two-fifths of what is required to be successful as a pastor. You must understand,” he said, “the inter-relationship of not only the preacher and the teacher, but the elder and the bishop and the shepherd.”

Not only the fivefold responsibility of the office of a pastor, but you taught me also how to Biblically fund the church. We come to the weekly stewardship sermonettes on storehouse tithing.

These two things, Dr. Clearwaters, are a legacy that you gave to me and that has stayed me down through nearly one quarter of a century in ministering to others.

The other part of the Scripture verse says: “. . . the same commit thou to faithful men, who shall be able to teach others also.” There are very few men in this nation listed in the Marquis “Who’s Who in America”. Very few pastors have ever attained this particular position in history. I think that most of us here at Fourth, at Central, and at Pillsbury have never fully understood and appreciated the tremendous stature of Dr. Richard V. Clearwaters and the impact that all the multi-faceted extensions of this pulpit ministry has made across the nation. Few really understand the history we have been shaking hands with each time we leave the auditorium.

I count it a privilege to have simply been here all those years. It had an impact on me, but not upon me only. Dr. Clearwaters, I thought about all the men who have passed through these doors, men who worked with us in the youth ministry of this church. We could name man after man after man; I am only a representative of all of these.

Dr. Clearwaters, you wrote a forward to a booklet we produced entitled, *A Youth Program that Works.* You penned these words:

> “At the 18th Annual Fellowship of the Conservative Baptist Association of America, which was meeting in the Memorial

> Coliseum of Portland Oregon, on May 27, 1961, the Youth Program of the Fourth Baptist Church was presented to the messengers.
>
> "The first Saturday was announced as vacating the Association Program to allow all Messengers to enjoy recreation and pleasure trips.
>
> "We took the opportunity on Saturday, made a dynamic ten-minute announcement and over 600 people, young and old, packed the auditorium."

Notice the word "we". If the pastor is not for the youth program, there will not be any youth program. It is the extension of the pulpit, which must be the dynamic center of the church. I'll never forget, Dr. Clearwaters, I came into your study one day, and I said, "Dr. Clearwaters, I've got a problem." You said, "We've got a problem, now what is it?" That was the rapport we enjoyed with him. There were many, many times I caused you a lot of problems. And somehow you always pulled me out!

I could add to Dr. Moritz' summary of statements. The Doc always said, "I'm the budget boy. You men on the staff always remember that." I will always remember it. I had to be reminded sometimes. As Mrs. Clearwaters reminded me one time in my home in Fort Lauderdale, "I heard the Doc explaining that to you one time as I was outside the door." Yes, I remember that very well.

Maybe some of you will remember my transportation problem. One day I walked down the street and found a hearse—$149.00 for this hearse—with wall-to-wall carpeting and blue lights! But I didn't have a chance to ask the Doc about it. I came driving up to the back here, and I thought now how will I tell the Doc what I've done. I've got to figure out something. This was not too long after the famous lecture I had about the budget. As I was driving up and thinking now what can I say, how can I justify this, out the door came Dr. Clearwaters. No place to hide; be sure your sins will find you out! Then I thought to myself there's one haven here. He's always saying, if you make a mistake, be sure it's on the side of the angels!

We've enjoyed having Dr. and Mrs. Clearwaters down in Florida with us year after year, and it has been nothing but a blessing to sit in consultation with him. Dr. Clearwaters, you penned this note in 1982 in my Bible: "Our ministry for Christ could never have been so glorious and blessed without our dedicated wives, Florence and Grace." Believe me, behind every man who has ever moved anybody has stood his wife.

Thanks for times now but a memory,
Shall we pause for a time reminiscing
As the years that have passed are reviewed?
And the names and the places forgotten
Are once again brought into view?
For many years I've been privileged
At the side of the only pastor I ever had
To work. He has taught me the code of the soldier
And never from duty to shirk.

Thank you, Dr. Clearwaters, not just for myself and my wife, but for that inumerable number of young people that you privileged me to impact for you for Jesus Christ.

Dr. Joseph Rammel: It is a tremendous privilege for me and my wife to be able to be present tonight. Dr. and Mrs. Clearwaters, we would travel many, many miles to be here. We are still in Owatonna, and it's a pleasure to be here on this particular occasion.

At the college I have always told our faculty that when you are employed, your wife is as much a part of the ministry of Pillsbury Baptist Bible College as the husband who is drawing the paycheck. I know that is also the case here at Fourth Baptist Church and Central Seminary. Mrs. Clearwaters, they are not going to call you President Emeritus of Central Baptist Theological Seminary, but actually it is a team effort, and Dr. Clearwaters could vouch for this, I'm sure, that Mrs. Clearwaters has been a vital part of this ministry and all of his ministry through the years. So many times the stories are never told of what the wife goes through. We appreciate her, and so I would like to address remarks to Dr. and Mrs. Clearwaters.

First of all, I wonder how many here tonight either graduated from or attended Pillsbury College. Would you please stand? And those who have attended or graduated from Central Seminary, will you stand with these? Dr. and Mrs. Clearwaters, you can see even here the product of the ministries that you have had a vital part in. In fact, if it were not for Dr. and Mrs. Clearwaters I doubt that either of these institutions would be in existence. Thank you very much for standing.

I did not have the privilege of being a student of Dr. Clearwaters at Central Seminary or at Pillsbury College. But I have been a student of his privately in a number of ways. How I wish I could have had many of our conversations recorded so that I could listen over and over again. I have appreciated them, and I have tried to identify ten aspects of the influence of Dr. Clearwaters upon American fundamentalism (which has also been a direct influence in my own personal life).

Quickly in outline form: first, his pastorate—the testimony of Fourth Baptist Church, one of the most tremendous churches in the entire world, and the manner in which Dr. Clearwaters pastored the church. There was always a balance in his ministry.

Second, his expository preaching—what an impact his expository preaching has been and the fact that he speaks the truth and earnestly contends for the faith. He had a way of making "accordion" messages, adjusted according to the situation and time!

Third, his doctrine—A Biblical Baptist position and an eschatology of pre-millenial pre-tribulational rapture as the blessed hope of the church.

Fourth, his Baptistic separatism—I appreciate a man who will stand up without compromise on a Biblical separatistic position, ecclesiastical separation from apostasy and personal separation from worldliness.

Fifth, his pen—you have seen all the pamphlets and books and booklets he has written and tremendous power and influence by use of his pen.

Sixth, his finances—I don't know very much about his personal finances, but in terms of the finances of the physical plant here and knowing how to work with deacons and trustees to bring about the kind of facility on this corner. In addition to that, he emphasizes stewardship in such a marvelous way so that people know they are supposed to give, are compelled to give and want to give.

Seventh, his example in education—this to me has been a tremendous impact. I realize there would not be a Pillsbury College if it had not been for Dr. Clearwaters. His own education, a professor and teacher himself, in addition to that as the founder of the various educational institutions, such as the Christian Day School, the Bible Institute program, Central Baptist Theological Seminary and Pillsbury Baptist Bible College, just to name a few of the main ones. Of course, his philosophy in education of direct presentation of divine truths versus an indirect method where only relative truths prevail.

Eighth, his practical practice—I call it practical practice because he is a practical person and believes in making things practical so somebody like me can understand. He uses poems, illustrations and that forever, "for instance".

Ninth, his insight into the world of ideas—spiritual, economic and political. A spiritual principle, for example, of religious freedom and faith that only free, independent autonomous local churches can really safeguard this America that we so enjoy. His economic principle, the value of capitalism and the value of free enterprise. And politically, the representative government and the importance of it in our democracy.

Tenth, his tremendous leadership—so many of his sayings are indelibly in our memory. He resigned from the Board of the Northern Baptist Seminary and said, "The chains of ecclesiastical bondage are too weak to be felt until they are too strong to be broken." Another, "A man is known by his enemies—not just by his friends." Another, "Work through channels." This is tremendous when one is dealing with leadership. Another, "Take the long look." You've heard these many times.

Yes, Dr. Clearwaters is truly the dean of Biblical separatism. It was about nineteen years ago that I first met him. Seventeen of these years I've had the privilege of working with him in a very unique way, not as his student and not as a member of his local church; but in spite of my age, thirty plus years difference between us, and yet Dr. Clearwaters always treated me as his equal. I never felt capable of that and I always appreciated that respect, and it made me respect him that much more. We have an unusual love relationship of appreciation. I know where he stood all the time, and I think he knew where I stood at the same time, and we stood together. Some of the greatest years that Pillsbury College ever experienced were during the term that Dr. Clearwaters was President and then Chairman of the Board of Trustees.

I talked to Doc many times when things didn't always look rosy and there were particular concerns and problems. He reminded me often of the Central Seminary logo of the picture of the ox on the fire of sacrifice and the yoke. When I think of self-sacrifice, I know that Dr. Clearwaters has said to me, "Joe, if I had to be sacrificed, I'm willing and I'm ready."

I certainly have appreciated all of the rich times we have had together. God only made one mold of a Clearwaters. When he made that one, he threw it away; there is no more. What a privilege we have had to be a part of his ministry.

Rev. Bruce Henry: I just want to read a few verses, but before I do, I just had a real encouraging comment by Mrs. Clearwaters. She leaned over and she said, "At least there's one young person up here." She had her eyes closed or she wasn't looking at my gray hair.

Please allow me to read a few verses in II Timothy chapter 2, which I think aptly portray Dr. Clearwaters. Paul says to Timothy, "Thou therefore endure hardness, as a good soldier of Jesus Christ. No man that warreth entangleth himself with the affairs of this life; that he may please him who hath chosen him to be a soldier."

It is indeed a real privilege for me to give testimony of the influence of Dr. Clearwaters, not in my life only, but in the lives of some of the Central graduates across our land.

It was a real blessing for me the past several weeks to call dozens of alumni of Central Baptist Seminary and to ask them about the influence Dr. Clearwaters has had on their life and on their ministry. I trust it will be a blessing to you as well.

Almost five hundred graduates have passed through the halls of this institution and graduated. I contacted many from all across the nation. I tried to get to some foreign countries. I called graduates from every decade of graduation, almost from every year of graduation from this institution, from many walks of life. I spoke to those who knew Dr. Clearwaters well, quite intimately, as well as those who knew him only as a professor or as a pastor.

Many responded with this statement: "Dr. Clearwaters was the single greatest human influence for me in the ministry." What a testimony, Doc, to have those say that about you. I asked the alumni what was it about Dr. Clearwaters in his ministry or in his life that really motivated you or helped you or is helping you now. I compiled all the thoughts I gathered over the past several weeks. I came down to five things in his ministry alone.

One was his preaching. So many men looked to his preaching as a great example for them. I only heard him in his prime, from 1977 on, but many heard him much before that, and they said preaching was one of the greatest assets of his ministry.

The second area was church administration. All of my pithy statements have been taken already by Dr. Moritz, but let me share a couple more. "More men will fail in the ministry in administration than in anything else." He also said, "It is important to surround yourself with good men." And another of his sayings which I have truly taken to heart recently, "Handle the mail only once."

Dr. and Mrs. R.V. Clearwaters, 1986.

Third, he had an influence in the area of separation. Men said this about Dr. Clearwaters, "An unquestioning black and white stand in spite of all the compromises of my friends and others." He also said this in regard to separation, he "was concerned for the purity of God's Word in God's Church."

Dr. Clearwaters has had an influence on others in preaching, in administration, in his separation in his church as well as his personal life. Also, he had an influence in his Baptist convictions and his heritage. Many men mentioned that.

And finally, his love for the ministry. As II Timothy chapter 2 mentions, "This one thing I do." It's important to concentrate on that one thing, the ministry.

Then I asked the alumni regarding the man. How did Dr. Clearwaters himself personally encourage you; how was he an example to you? They said his self-discipline was the most popular thing. They saw him here early in the morning when they came to school, and they saw him working many late hours, working on Saturdays and working every day of the week. They also said his love and his time for people of all ages was an encouragement to them. It was so exciting to talk with the alumni, some of those long-distance phone calls became long, as they shared with me how Dr. Clearwaters had taken time for their children or had taken time for those with physical disabilities and those with other problems. His boundless energy was another area of comment.

Faithfulness, perseverence, stability in his own personal life were tremendous examples to many graduates. Many men shared with me that Dr. Clearwaters had led them to Jesus Christ; Dr. Clearwaters had baptized them; Dr. Clearwaters had performed their marriage; Dr. Clearwaters had been instrumental in encouraging them to go into the ministry, being their friend and counsellor, being their example during the formative years of their Christian life and ministry. When they would call back for advice, he was their counsellor.

The graduates that I talked to wanted to say thank you. I have a list of several areas which I compiled of statements of thanks to Dr. Clearwaters:

"I thank you, Doc, for sharing your passion for studying God's Word." I guess a statement he said often was that if I quit studying, I'll know the next day, and my people will know the next service.

"Thank you, Dr. Clearwaters, for your faithful leadership."

"Thank you for being a friend and counsellor."

"Thank you for being an example of a servant." The stories I heard were just tremendous of things Dr. Clearwaters would often do which other people could have done.

"Thank you for inspiring me to go into the ministry."

"Thank you, Doc, for your consistency."

And one that I could add: "Thank you for your vision to establish Pillsbury Baptist Bible College and Central Baptist Seminary so that God could multiply your ministry throughout the world."

Will you consider with me for just a moment the institutions of Biblical learning in our nation and world—the Bible colleges and the seminaries. Then consider the leaders of those institutions—the presidents, administration, faculty and staff. Then consider where many of these leaders received their training. For many of the leaders across our land, Central Seminary was one of those institutions. I had the privilege of talking to one of the presidents of a Bible college in our nation, a graduate of Central Baptist Seminary, and he wanted to share a statement with those who would be in the audience this evening. And these are his words: "I have always been grateful for the good solid training in Biblical studies in theology that I received at Central Seminary, and for the impact of Dr. Clearwaters upon my life. His wit, his wisdom, his vitality, his diligence gave me excitement and enthusiasm toward the ministry. His strong stand on issues helped to sharpen my awareness to likewise be strong in the Lord and in the power of His might." I can say "amen" to that as well.

I personally would like to say thank you to Dr. Clearwaters for his example in my life and in my ministry. Thank you for your positive impact on the lives of so many, and I pray every day, as you have prayed so many times, "Lord, make me to do better than I know."

I also want to thank Dr. Clearwaters for his vision to establish these schools of Biblical learning. A poem entitled, "Building the Bridge for Him" by W.A. Dromgoole concludes my testimony:

An old man going down a long highway
Came at the evening, cold and gray,
To a chasm vast and deep and wide.
The old man crossed in the twilight dim;
The sullen stream had no fears for him.
But he turned when safe on the other side
And built a bridge to span the tide.
"Old man," said a fellow pilgrim near,

"You're wasting your time with building here.
You never again will pass this way;
You've crossed the chasm, deep and wide.
Why build you this bridge at eventide?"
The builder lifted his old gray head.
"Good friend, in the way I've come," he said,
"There followeth after me today a youth
Whose feet must pass this way.
This stream that has been as naught to me
To the fair-haired youth might a pitfall be.
He, too, must cross in the twilight dim.
Good friend, I'm building this bridge for him."

God bless you, Dr. Clearwaters.

CHAPTER 11

Separation of the Individual Christian and the Local Church

A well-known evangelist of our day whose ministry is almost "sloganized" by the phrase "The Bible Says" has authored a tract published by the American Tract Society on the subject "Worldliness and Separation." This evangelist speaks of worldliness and separation in the following words:

> "God calls us to be a separated people: 'Come out from among them, and be ye separate' (II Corinthians 6:17). . . What is worldliness actually?
>
> "A prominent writer described it very aptly: 'It is the self-indulgent attitude of the heart and mind towards life.' It is not merely doing certain forbidden things or going to certain prescribed

> places. Worldliness is what we are, not just what we do. It is in reality an inner attitude, for as man 'thinketh in his heart, so is he' (Proverbs 23:7). Any Christian whose interest is directed toward himself is worldly."

Our only comment on the above use of Scripture is to finish the quotation where the evangelist stopped at a comma and let the evangelist's use of his text be condemned by his context. We simply remark, "The Bible Says" "Come out from among them, and be ye separate," and in the same connection as we continue the inspired sentence, "The Bible Says," "And touch not the unclean thing; and I will receive you." The evangelist's text nor context say anything about "Be ye separate in your heart!" What the Bible says in this connection is primarily with, not the *internal environment* but with the *external environment* of these New Testament Christians.

> "Vice is a monster of so frightful mien,
> As to be hated needs but to be seen;
> Yet seen too oft, familiar with her face
> We first endure, then pity, then embrace."

(*Essay on Man*, Epistle II, line 1, by Alexander Pope)

The Principles of Separation Throughout the Bible

Jude's theme, "contending for the faith" treats the cause and course of apostasy, and in verse eleven warns the church of the ages against a false Religion, a false Ministry, and a false Worship in these words, "Woe to them! for they have gone in the *way of Cain*, and ran greedily after the *error of Balaam* for reward, and perished in the *gainsaying of Core*."

II Timothy and II Peter warn the church:

1. against the apostasy of the false profession of the unsaved calling themselves Christians;
2. against the apostasy of false teachers originating apostasy;
3. and against the false doctrines of false teachers who deny the twin truths of Redemption and Christ's Person.

An honest exposition and application of Exodus chapters 8-10 shows God's warning against apostasy in the Old Testament. After Israel's Moses rejected the *counterfeit* (Exodus 7:11) and refused the *compro-*

mises (Exodus 8:25-29; Exodus 10:8-11), Moses faced with Israel the same alternative the true visible church faces today: "Separation or Compromise"! The world will long remember Moses' decision and has long forgotten the compromising collaborationists. Satan's last resort in strategy was then, as now, open *conflict* (Exodus 14:1-16).

Deuteronomy 22:9-11 is the next great test of Israel's keeping a pure testimony in which God warns Israel against *mixed seeds* of teaching which defile; *mixed service* of believers and unbelievers; and against *mixed conduct* represented by the garment of woolen and linen. God here condemns the present-day custom of mixing Scripture with science, Scripture with sociology, Scripture with politics, Scripture with psychology, Scripture with philosophy, art and so forth that has been the ruin of the modern pulpit. God knows only too well that the soil of fallen hearts, predisposed to evil, will grow the secular seeds more rankly than the sacred seeds, if both be sown together.

God's second warning is against *mixed service*: "Thou shalt not plow with an ox (a clean animal) and an ass (an unclean animal) together." God's soil is not only to be sown solely with God's seed, but His plow also must be drawn only by His servant. The deliberate choice of a partner or colleague God makes very important; in marriage for domestic ends; in business for commercial ends; in friendship for social ends; in religion for Christian and church ends—God forbids an unbeliever to be in the team.

God warns against *mixed conduct*: "Thou shalt not wear a garment of divers sorts, *as* of woolen and linen together." Conduct expresses a man's character precisely as his clothes outline the contour of his body. Scripture likewise consistently uses clothing as figurative of conduct. Linen in Scripture is always the holy fabric (Revelation 19:8). It is the only textile fabric the priesthood were allowed to wear (Ezekiel 44:17). The saved all belong to the priesthood of believers.

The best scholars have considered that, as literature, the New Testament was *occasioned* by four notable events or movements:

1. the Greek Mission, or the evangelization of the Gentile world;
2. the fall of Jerusalem as prophesied in the Old Testament is interpreted as history in the New Testament;
3. the church is bracing itself against the persecution of Domitian;
4. the church is plunged into controversy over its own beliefs because of

the rise of early sects.

In considering this last division of New Testament literature any good analysis provides principles of separation with undisputed and inspired divine authority and illustration. Thus we identify our theme and thesis with the historic New Testament Christianity that we accept as our model and guide.

There will always be those who are willing to give aid or sympathy to the enemy who will be caustic or critical, and there will be those who will give heartfelt and sincere commendation to these stern and strong Bible teachings on this doctrine of *Bible separation.*

A dangerous progression becomes evident as we consider the philosophy of infiltration versus separation.

1. *Identification* with evil: Webster's definition—"To make to be the same; to consider as the same in any relation; to establish identity of or to prove the same."
2. *Federation* with evil: Webster's definition—"A uniting by league and covenant especially in forming a sovereign power so that each of the uniting powers retains local powers."
3. *Collaboration* with evil: Webster's definition—"Laborers working together."
4. *Amalgamation* with evil: Webster's definition—"To combine into a uniform whole."
5. *Subjugation* to evil: Webster's definition—"To bring under the yoke of power or dominion; reduce to subjection or submission; to make subservient; something joined."

Note the warnings in the letter to Ephesus (4:12-30): *Mental Darkness*, "This I say therefore, and testify in the Lord, that ye henceforth walk not as other Gentiles walk, in the vanity of their mind, *Having the understanding darkened"; Spiritual Death, "being alienated from the life of God* through the ignorance that is in them, because of the blindness of their heart". *Moral Degeneracy,* "Who being *past feeling* . . . "; and *Physical Depravity*, "have given themselves over unto lasciviousness, to work all uncleanness with greediness. But ye have not so learned Christ";

Throughout the ages God's method has never been federation with evil, but separation from evil!

The Application of Biblical Principles of Separation

I. *The separated life for the individual member of the local church:*

a. Does the thought, deed, or act in question enslave me? "All things are lawful unto me, but all things are not expedient: all things are lawful unto me, but I will not be brought under the power of any." (I Corinthians 6:12)

b. Does the thought, deed, or act in question build me up (physically, mentally, spiritually)? "All things are lawful for me, but all things are not expedient: all things are lawful for me, but all things edify not." (I Corinthians 10:23)

c. Does the matter in question cause others to stumble? "But when ye sin so against the brethren, and wound their weak conscience, ye sin against Christ. Wherefore, if meat make my brother to offend, I will eat no flesh while the world standeth, lest I make my brother to offend." (I Corinthians 8:12-13)

d. Does the matter in question glorify God? "Whether therefore ye eat, or drink, or whatsoever ye do, do all to the glory of God." (I Corinthians 10:31)

e. Are the things in question doubtful: "And he that doubteth is damned if he eat, because *he eateth* not of faith: for whatsoever is not of faith is sin." (Romans 14:23), e.g. "These six *things* doth the LORD hate: yea, seven *are* an abomination unto him: A proud look, a lying tongue, and hands that shed innocent blood, An heart that deviseth wicked imaginations, feet that be swift in running to mischief, A false witness *that* speaketh lies, and he that soweth discord among brethren." (Proverbs 6:16-19)

II. *The separated position for the local church;* Acts 14, 15.

a. Disciplining members who live in open sin (Matthew 18:15, 17; I Corinthians 5:1; II Thessalonians 3:1-6; Titus 3:10, 11).

b. Electing to office only members who live a separated life (Acts 6:3-7).

c. Employing only Sunday school teachers who live a separated life and bear a strong testimony (II Timothy 2:1-3).

d. Refusing nonchurch members to teach or hold office (Matthew 18:17, I Corinthians 5:1, II Corinthians 2:5-11).

e. Refusing unbiblical programs in the local church (Acts 2:42).
f. Accepting only sound missionaries and missionary objectives in the local church (Acts 2:42).
g. Intolerance of unbiblical pastors (Jude 11).
h. Refusal by majority of local church to authorize or send messengers to any unorthodox ecclesiastical organization or institution (Acts 14, 15).
i. Refusal of local church to receive or recognize unregenerate and unbaptized members in local church (I Timothy 1:18-20).
j. Refusal of local church to welcome or allow any individual in church pulpit of questionable orthodoxy or any person of questionable orthodoxy to be presented or sponsored (I Timothy 1:18-20).
k. The local church preaching the true biblical gospel in the pulpit should refuse that any other gospel be allowed to be taught in the Sunday school or supported in any auxiliary organization bearing the name of the church.
l. The church should depend for its financial support of all objectives solely upon tithes and offerings and should be vocal against all commercial means and schemes of raising money (I Corinthians 16:1, 2; Matthew 23:23).

Conclusion

To be absolutely accurate historically, when we insist upon a strict biblical witness in Christianity we are neither proposing nor practicing separation! We are *restoring* "the faith once for all delivered" where it has been lost; we are *reconstructing* this faith where it is deficient, we are *reviving* it where it is dormant. These principles have been recognized in many courts of law.

Perhaps the greatest menace to fundamental Christianity today is a part of its leadership which professes to be fundamental under the name of the New Evangelicalism but at the same time they hate the word separation like poison, usually for two reasons. First, because they want to be *inclusivists* and be yoke-fellows with Modernists and Liberals in the salvation of the lost and in the service of the church; and second, they hate the word separation because they want to walk with one foot in the path of the Christian and one in the path of the worldling. It is still true that the finest of the wheat in our Prayer Meeting crowd are not found at the card table, among the regular patrons of the theater, and among those who are fond of the dance.

We began this treatise with a sharp disagreement with a modern-day Evangelist who would misinterpret the Word of God in order to retain his popularity with a pleasure-loving, compromising, and worldly public. We close the treatise by quoting an illustration from a great sermon, "Overcoming the World" by William Edward Biederwolf, who was the father in the ministry of Evangelist "Billy Sunday". (These men were both fearless, modern prophets in proclaiming the "whole council of God", BOTH POSITIVE AND NEGATIVE):

Sunday golf tournaments, Sunday baseball, and Sunday night dances all claim a plentiful number of professing Christians among their patrons. Prize-winning bridge parties are quite the thing nowadays among church members who twenty-five years ago would have shaken their heads in resolute disapproval; and to these and other forms of indulgence, either questionable or admittedly unholy, professing Christians have been giving themselves to such a degree that today we find ourselves with a church going on crutches, unable to stand erect and be the power for righteousness God meant her to be, because the world has been boring its way like a putrifying abscess into her very vitals, her very heart.

Listen to this conversation:

"Dick," said a young wife, "I've been a very happy woman for four years now, but if only one other thing could be, I think I'd be the happiest woman in the world."

"Well, Mollie, what is it? I'd do anything for you."

"Oh, Dick! If you were only a Christian!"

"Well, Mollie, are you a Christian?"

"Why, yes, Dick."

"Well, Mollie, I—didn't know it."

Dick went into a brown study for a moment and then said, "Mollie, you don't swear, do you?"

"No, Dick."

"Well, I don't either. Mollie, you don't steal do you?"

"No, Dick."

"Well, I don't either. And Mollie, you don't get drunk, do you?"

"Why, no Dick; of course I don't! Why do you ask me such questions?"

"Well, Mollie, you play cards, don't you, and for prizes?"

"Certainly, Dick; there's no harm in that."

"Well, Mollie, I do too."

"Mollie, you go to the theater, don't you?"

"Why, yes, Dick."

"Well, I do too. And Mollie, you drink wine, don't you?"

"Oh, yes; I do that out of courtesy to the hostess."

"Well, I do, too. And Mollie, you dance, don't you?"

"Why, yes; I love to dance."

"Well, Mollie, I do too. And now, Mollie, if you will tell me the difference between the kind of life you are living and the kind of life I am living, I think I would be willing to become a Christian, if there's any difference."

Listen! If the religion of Jesus Christ doesn't make any difference between the way you live and the way your unconverted friends or relatives live, it is not worth recommending to them as a religion for doing the things the religion of Jesus Christ is supposed to do. "He that is born of God overcometh the world."

Chapter 12

Biblicist Baptist *Faith and Practice*

Modernists have created what they think to be a better Christ than Jesus of Nazareth. A liberal contributed some time ago to a liberal magazine an article on the mistakes of Jesus. Orthodox believers are shocked at this departure from the Christian faith. And yet many orthodox believers in practice pride themselves in improving upon the Christianity of Christ by being more "tolerant", "kind", "loving", and "understanding" than was Jesus of Nazareth. There is a species of orthodox believers who have professed to accept the Christ of the faith, but in their practice of their species of Christianity they have departed from the Christianity of Christianlikeness.

When Thomas Jefferson realized that only a Declaration of Independence from the British crown could be a solution and the salvation for this country, he was able to get only fifty-six signers for that now world-famous document which was the authoritative idealism behind the Revolutionary War. Many like Dickinson from Pennsylvania, who refused to sign the Declaration of Independence and voted against it to the last, called themselves "olive branch men". What a nice name they gave themselves! Most of them confessed faith in the principles outlined by their leader when the long hours of discussion were held, but they refused flatly to practice the principles. They thought the country should still try to do business with George the III and Great Britain. Irrespective of the provocative action the British crown government might take, the "olive branch men" found excuses for their consciences for following an appeasement pathway whatever terms were demanded.

"Take, eat; this is my body, which is broken for you: this do in remembrance of me" (I Corinthians 11:24). Paul, in this Scripture, is teaching the Corinthians what Jesus was unfolding to His followers in the great "Bread of Life" discourse in John's Gospel. "Then Jesus said unto them, Verily, verily, I say unto you, Except ye eat the flesh of the Son of man, and drink his blood, ye have no life in you. Whoso eateth my flesh, and drinketh my blood, hath eternal life; and I will raise him up at the last day" (John 6:53, 54). Jesus was putting Himself into the passover feast as the Passover Lamb! He was teaching that His blood, and His blood alone, could atone for sin. But to Jesus' great sorrow, there were professed followers of His, as He stood before them in the flesh, who refused to accept Jesus' blood as an atonement for their sins; there were those in the band of professed followers who accepted Him as teacher, until He taught them that He was the Passover Lamb. Plainly we are told in John 6:60, "Many therefore of His disciples, when they had heard this, said, This is an hard saying; who can hear it?"

At this time, Jesus did not put His arm around them in their unbelief and assure them that it made little difference what their views were on this matter as long as they lived right, kept a good attitude, and stayed with the band. He plainly told them, "There are some of you that believe not," and in John 6:66 we read, "From that time many of his disciples went back and walked no more with him." In self-judgment, they did not just go away from Jesus' teaching, according to the record; but, realizing that His teaching and Jesus Himself were One—One with whom they were not in unity—they went away from Jesus Christ. Jesus then leaving them in the hands of God as they turned away from Him, turned to His loyal band that remained, and asked, "Will ye also go away?"

Doubtless there were those in His day who deplored the divisions among them with some such words as we hear in this day, "Why can't we forget these controversial things which divide us?" Instead of trying to find a common denominator that everyone would accept, Jesus went further and laid the same test upon the Twelve and was ready to say "Good-Bye" to some of them if found in unbelief.

Space does not permit detailed treatment of Jesus' deliverances against the Chief Priests, Scribes and Elders on the question of Jesus' authority. His polemic illustrations of the Two Unlike Sons, the Wicked Husbandman, and The Marriage Feast were obviously given *not to convince His enemies but to convict them of their sins.* Certain sentimental Christians today would have criticized Jesus by saying, "You cannot win your enemies by being so negative."

Jesus followed the same procedure trying to bring conviction of sin into the hearts of the Pharisees and the Herodians on the question of the tribute money. He dealt with the sinful Saducees' skepticism of the resurrection in the same manner and with the Scribes and Lawyers on the question of the Great Commandment.

"Nevertheless among the chief rulers also many believed on him; but because of the Pharisees they did not confess him, lest they should be put out of the synagogue: For they loved the praise of men more than the praise of God" (John 12:42, 43).

In our day, many who will not sign their names to a Confession of Faith, or stand up and vote, or open their mouths in testimony, or raise their voices in protest to the gravest heresy, are frequently protected by their friends who piously plead, "Let us be charitable with these because they are all right in their personal faith." According to our Scripture passage, the same could have been said about many of those in places of authority whose conspiracy of silence allowed Jesus to be crucified.

The rulers' personal faith in Christ was overcome by their personal fear of the Pharisees. Our Lord, in Matthew 10:32, makes the statement: "Whosoever therefore shall confess me before men, him will I confess also before my Father which is in heaven." Let us note the conjuctive adverb "therefore", signifying logical sequence, which in this usage constitutes a severe and sharp warning. A law of physical life is that atrophy is a consequence of disuse of a member of the body which causes it to cease to grow and wither away. *We must give out our Christian testimony or give it up!*

Let us notice that the man-fearing rulers of old were not without love for the praise of God any more than they were without faith in Christ. The tragedy of their condition was that they believed more on the Pharisees than they did on Christ, and they loved the praise of men more than the praise of God. In Revelation 2:2, the Church at Ephesus was praised in these words by the glorified Christ: "And thou hast tried them which say they are apostles, and are not, and hast found them liars." In II Timothy 3:5, the Lord's great Apostle speaks of this class of people in even more severe terms: "Having a form of godliness but denying the power thereof: from such turn away."

In considering our last point which reveals the rulers too weak in character to provide a vindication of Jesus Christ, who can ever know the difference it would have made if among the chief rulers where many believed on him a large company could have risen up and would have become vocal in their vindication of the Christ. Things today are very similar. In I Timothy 3:15, 16, Paul explains the necessity of the positive proclamation of the Gospel. This is followed in I Timothy 4:1-6 by the grave and great necessity of what we may call the negative vindication of the Gospel of Jesus Christ. We will list a few of the enemies of the Gospel with what they believed and what they did not believe as Paul saw it in his day:

> "Some shall depart from the faith."
> Some shall give "heed to seducing spirits."
> Some shall give heed to "doctrines of devils."
> Some shall be "speaking lies in hypocrisy."
> Some shall have "their conscience seared with a hot iron."
> Some shall preach and teach a substitute gospel (See verse 3).

Paul specifically charges every true minister of Jesus Christ to become vocal and to take up arms against these enemies of Christ and His Gospel, concluding by saying, "If thou put the brethren in remembrance of these things, thou shalt be a good minister of Jesus Christ, nourished up in the words of faith and of good doctrine, whereunto thou hast attained."

Nothing is quite so disgusting and damaging as the professing orthodox Christians of our day, especially in leadership, who would sit back and speak of Paul in this passage as "vindictive", as "negative", and as "sitting in judgment upon his brethren".

According to the dictionary to vindicate means "to assert or defend against anything that attacks; maintain successfully, as right; justify". Today we have a flood of self-seeking, self-serving, and self-preserving ministers of Christ who take refuge in a false and unscriptural excuse, "The Gospel does not need any defense." Such people simply have not read the New Testament, for example, in the book of Acts where Paul and his co-laborers defended the gospel vehemently against idolatry, philosophy, and the sophistries of the day. Such cowardly characters have not read carefully Paul's defense of the Gospel in his Corinthian correspondence in which he makes a heated attack openly decrying immorality, skepticism, and false profession in general. Such ministers of Christ who are more interested in their own personal future than they are in the present safety of the Gospel of Christ have not read Paul's defense and vindication of the Gospel against the Judaizers in the book of Galatians.

"Don't be negative" is the cry so common today, especially among those who are so weak that instead of taking a stand against something they are forced to find something upon which they may lean. Public health officials are very negative in their restrictions and warnings against disease when an epidemic is rampant. Sin is pictured in the Bible as a disease. Poor Paul would have been called very unChristian in this day by some of these soft-fingered and kid-gloved ministers who would call Paul "dogmatic", a "name-caller", and "unChristian". It is doubtful if any writer of the New Testament is more tender and winsome than the Apostle Paul when he is trying to convince a lost sinner that Jesus should be his Saviour. On the other hand, when the Apostle Paul preached or picked up his pen to convict blatant and self-willed souls who were rebellious to the plainly revealed will of God, he is perhaps the most negative and most dogmatic of all the New Testament writers. The tragedy of today is the many who decry the negative ministry who are trying by a positive ministry to convince the Gospel enemies of the error of their ways instead of first convicting these enemies of the Gospel of their sin.

Supplemental Sources of Material

Transcription of cassette tapes of sermons preached by Dr. Clearwaters:

"My Spiritual Birthday" Sunday Evening Service, December 9, 1979
"Personal Testimony" Seminary Chapel Services, December 10, 1975, April 30, 1979, December 9, 1981
"The Bibles in My Life" Sunday Morning Service, April 21, 1974
"My Training for the Ministry" Midweek Service, May 13, 1976
"A Definite Call: Pastor or Priest" January 18, 1972

Transcription of copyrighted video/audio tapes made by Dr. Donald E. Nelson and used with permission:

Interview with Dr. Clearwaters by Dr. Nelson and Dr. Richard Schermerhorn, February 8, 1983
Personal Testimony given at Bethany Baptist Church, Fort Lauderdale, Florida, February 9, 1986
Recognition Service at Fourth Baptist Church on April 4, 1982
Recognition Service at Central Baptist Seminary on April 6, 1987
Testimony of Mrs. Florence Clearwaters, Women's Luncheon at Pillsbury Baptist Bible College, 1986

Other Books Authored by Dr. R.V. Clearwaters

The Great Conservative Baptist Compromise, Central Seminary Press
The Ten Commandments, Central Seminary Press, 1975
The Local Church of the New Testament, Central Seminary Press
Stewardship Sermonettes
Stewardship Sermonettes II, 1975